PRETTY POND LIFE

&

REPTILES!

COLORING BOOK

Pretty POND LIFE Coloring Book

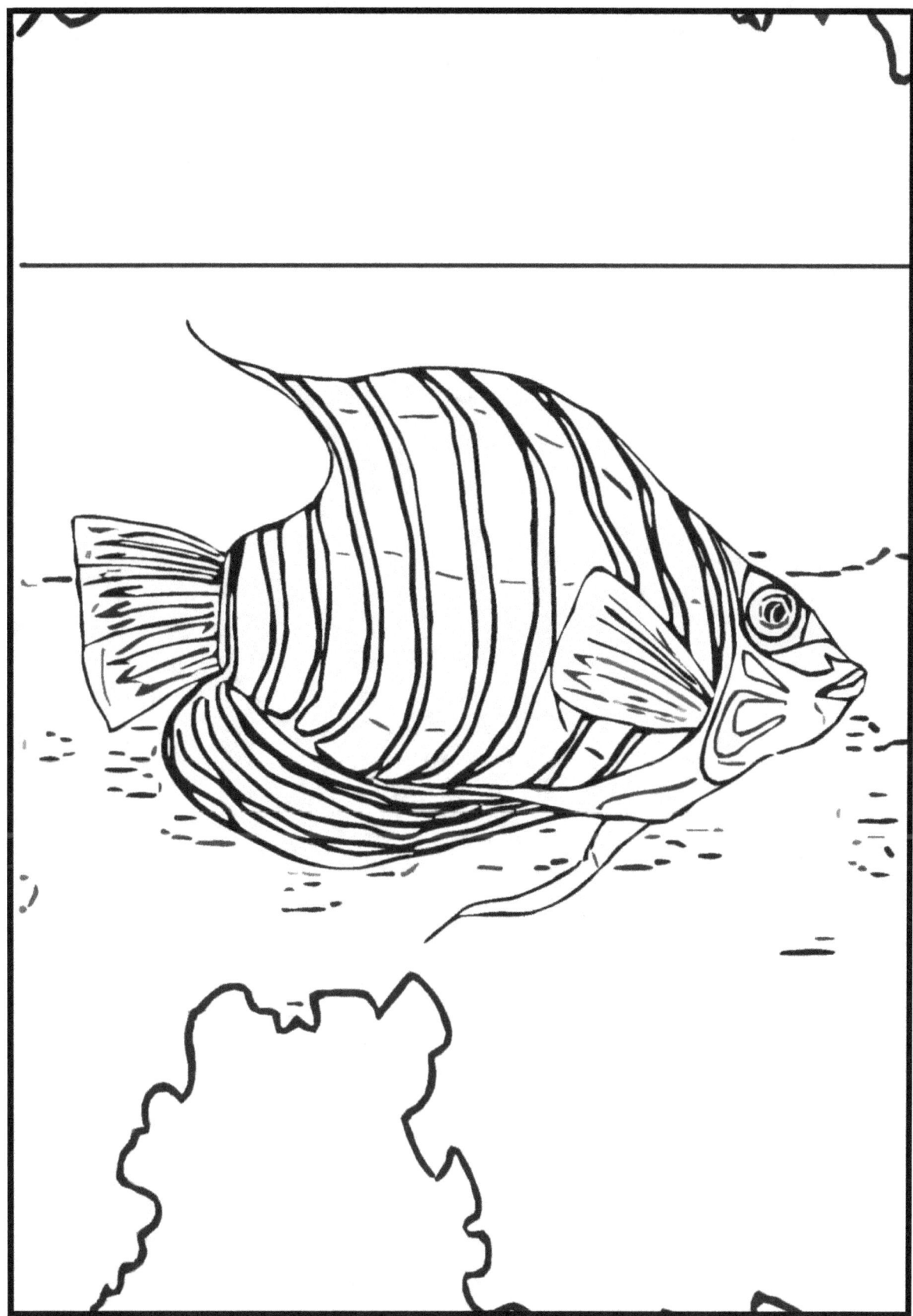

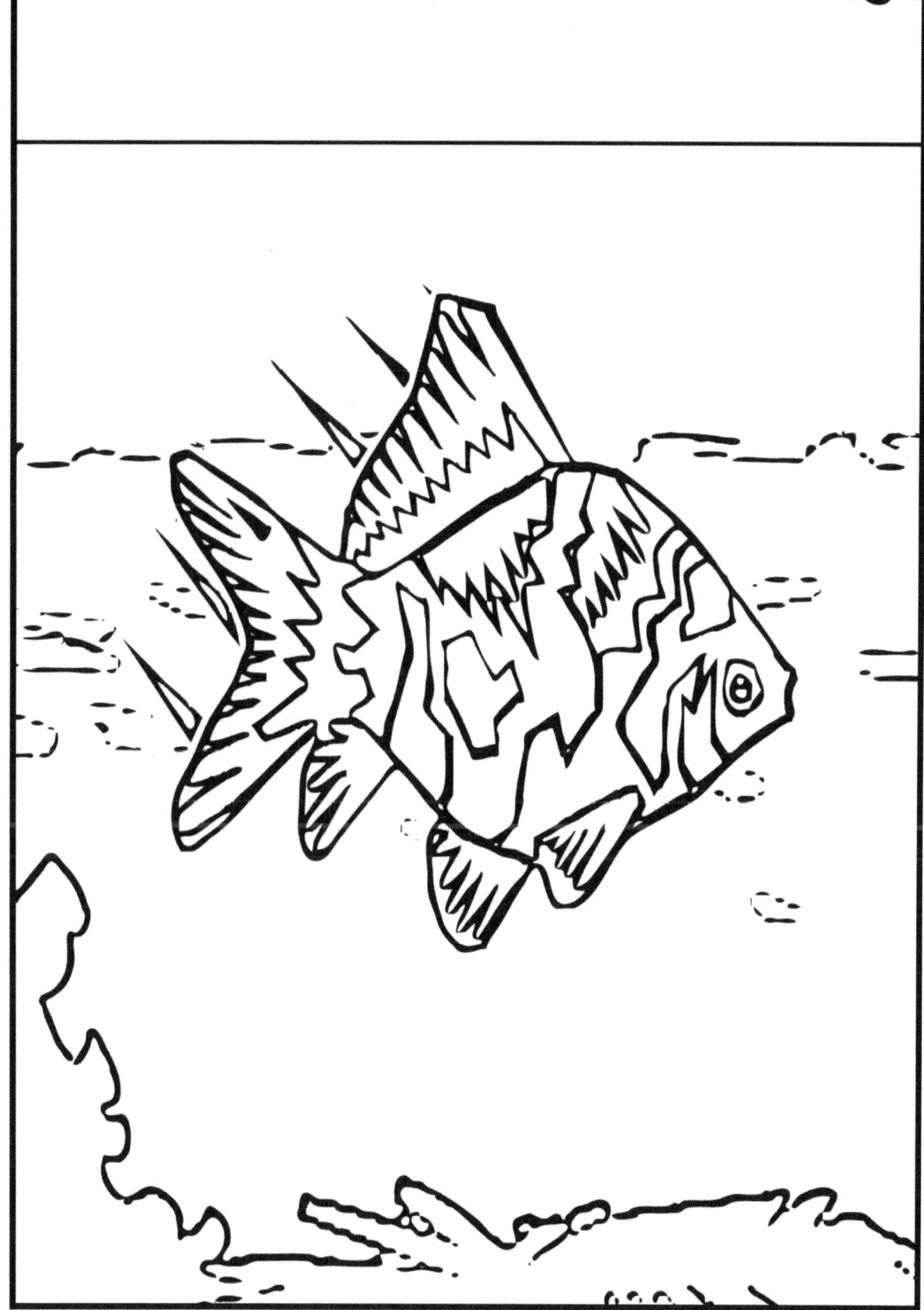

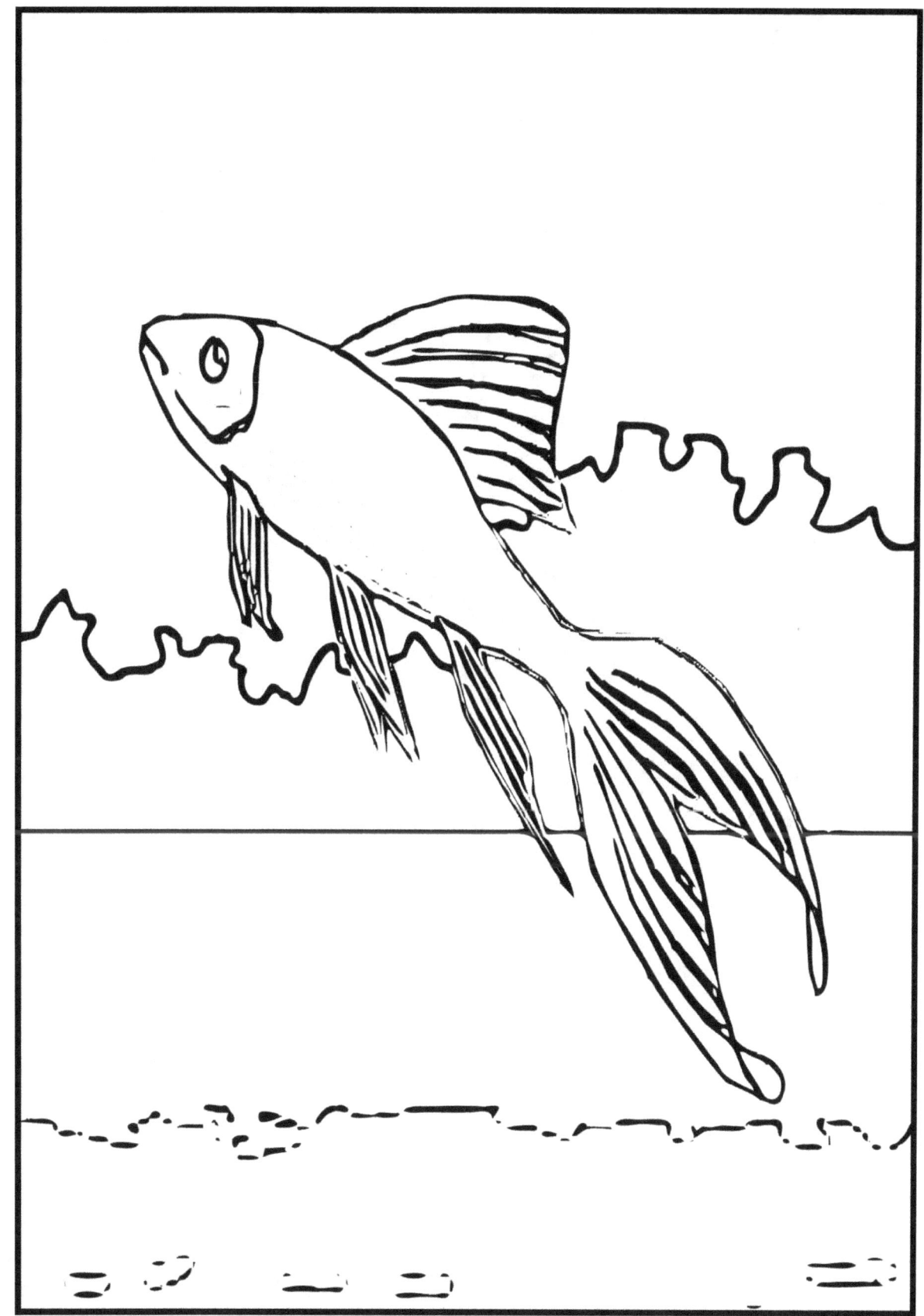

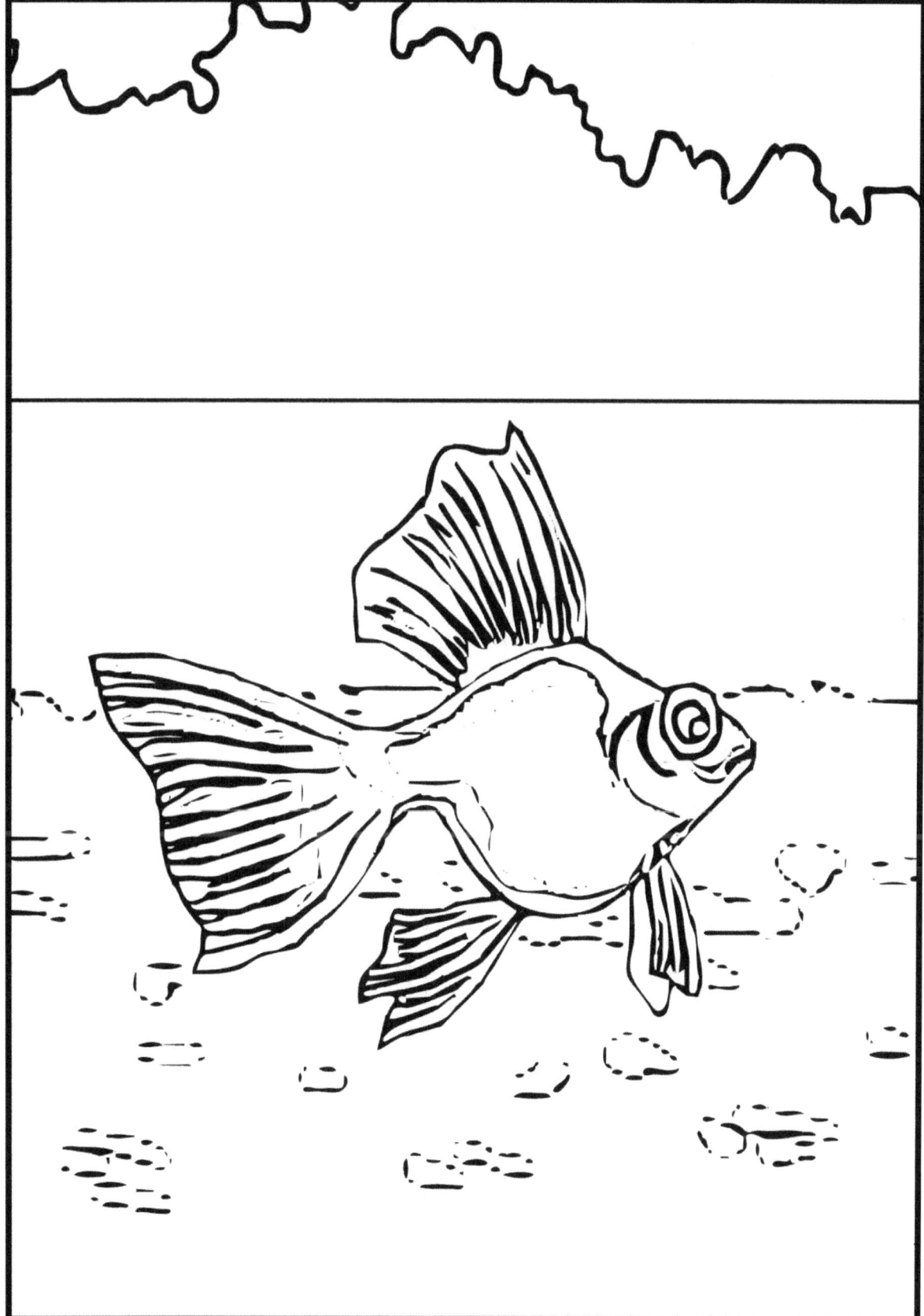

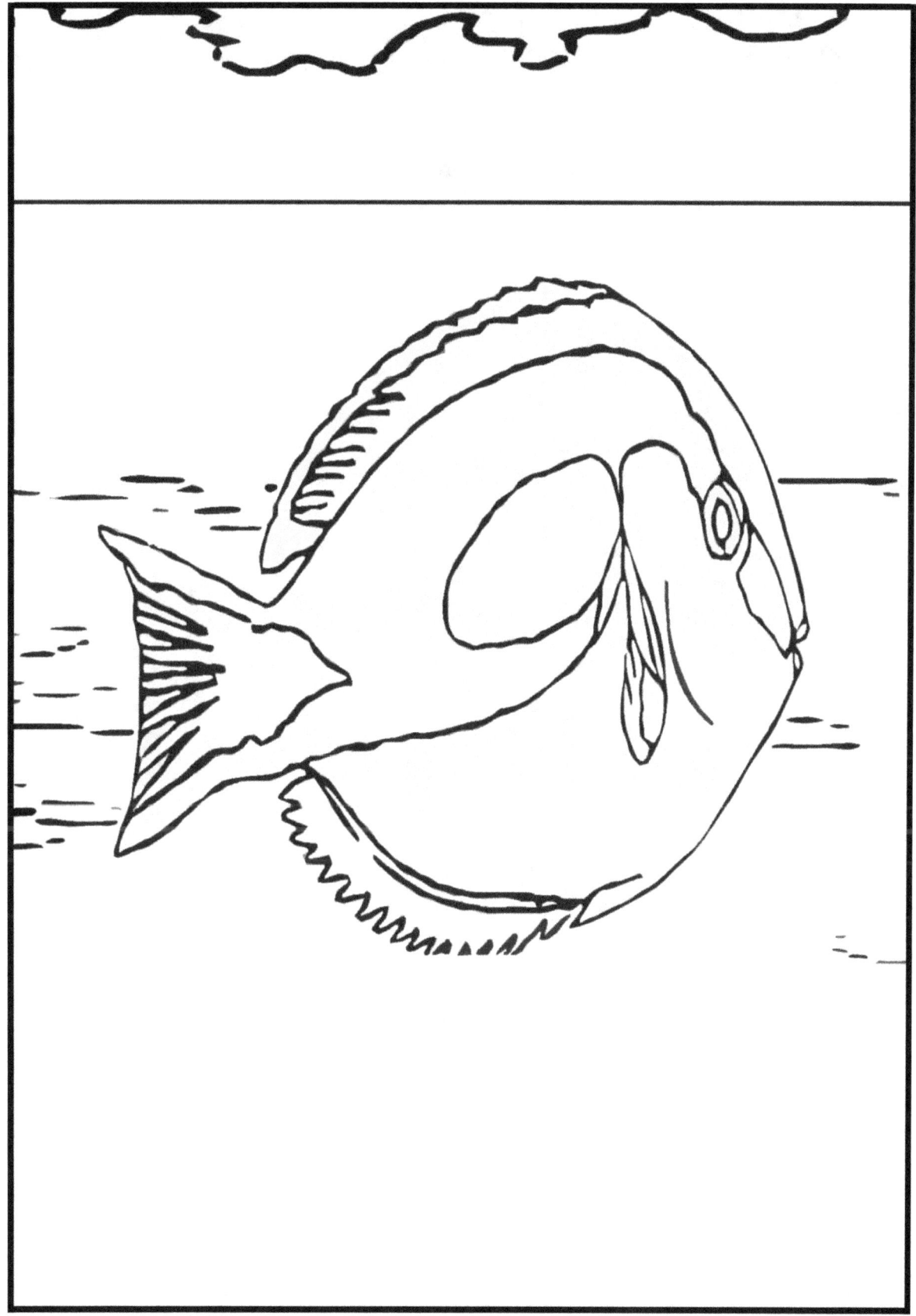

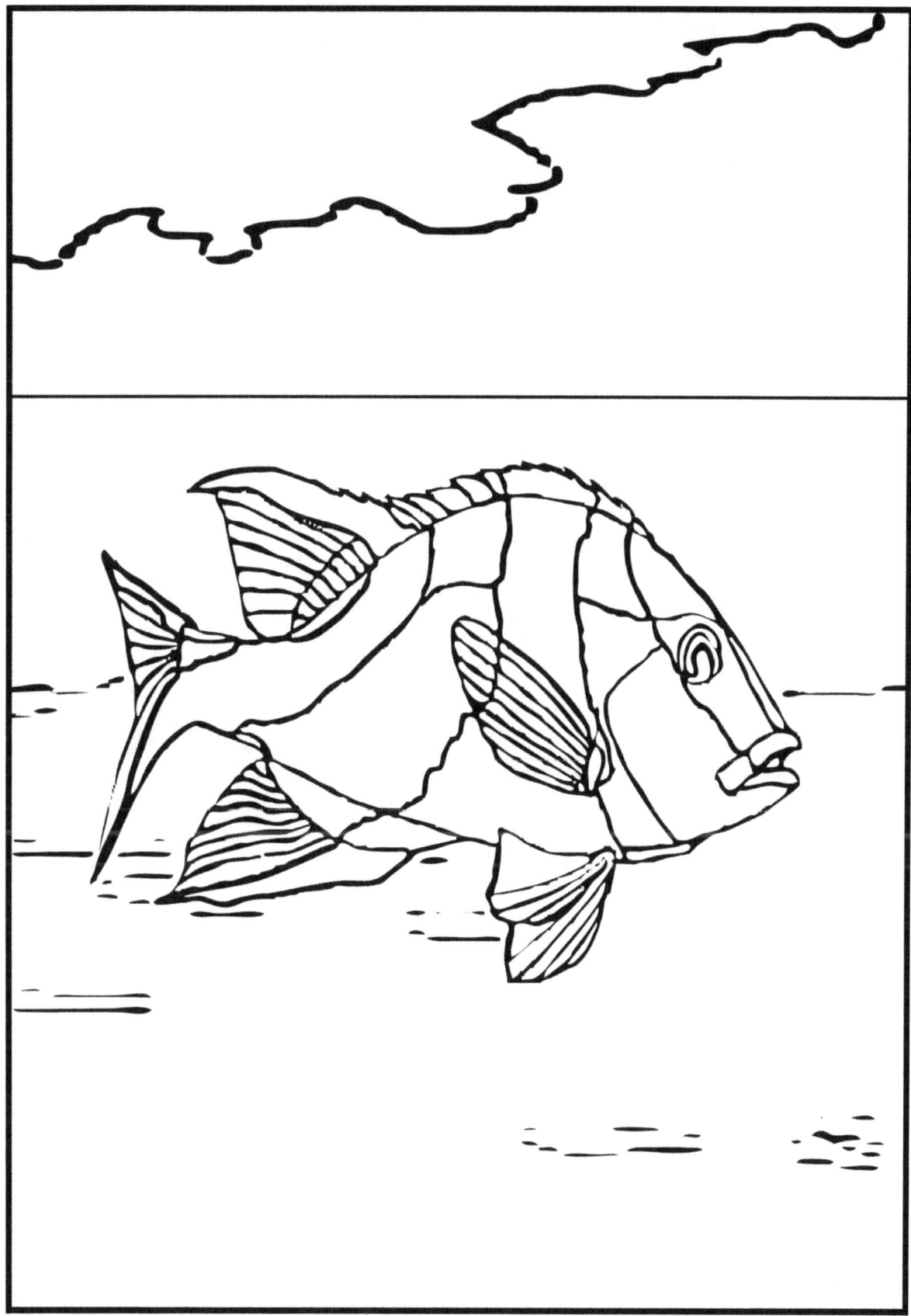

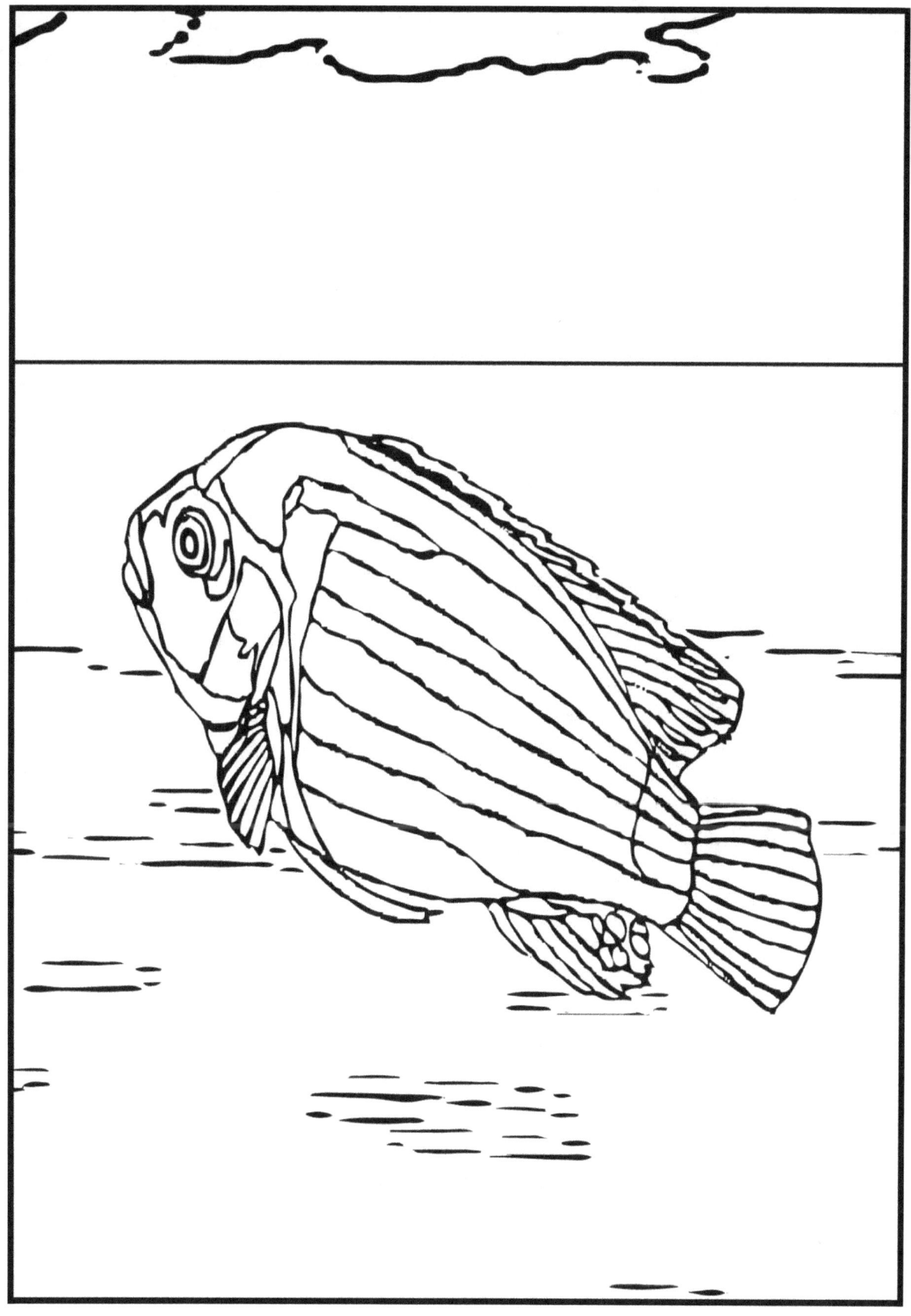

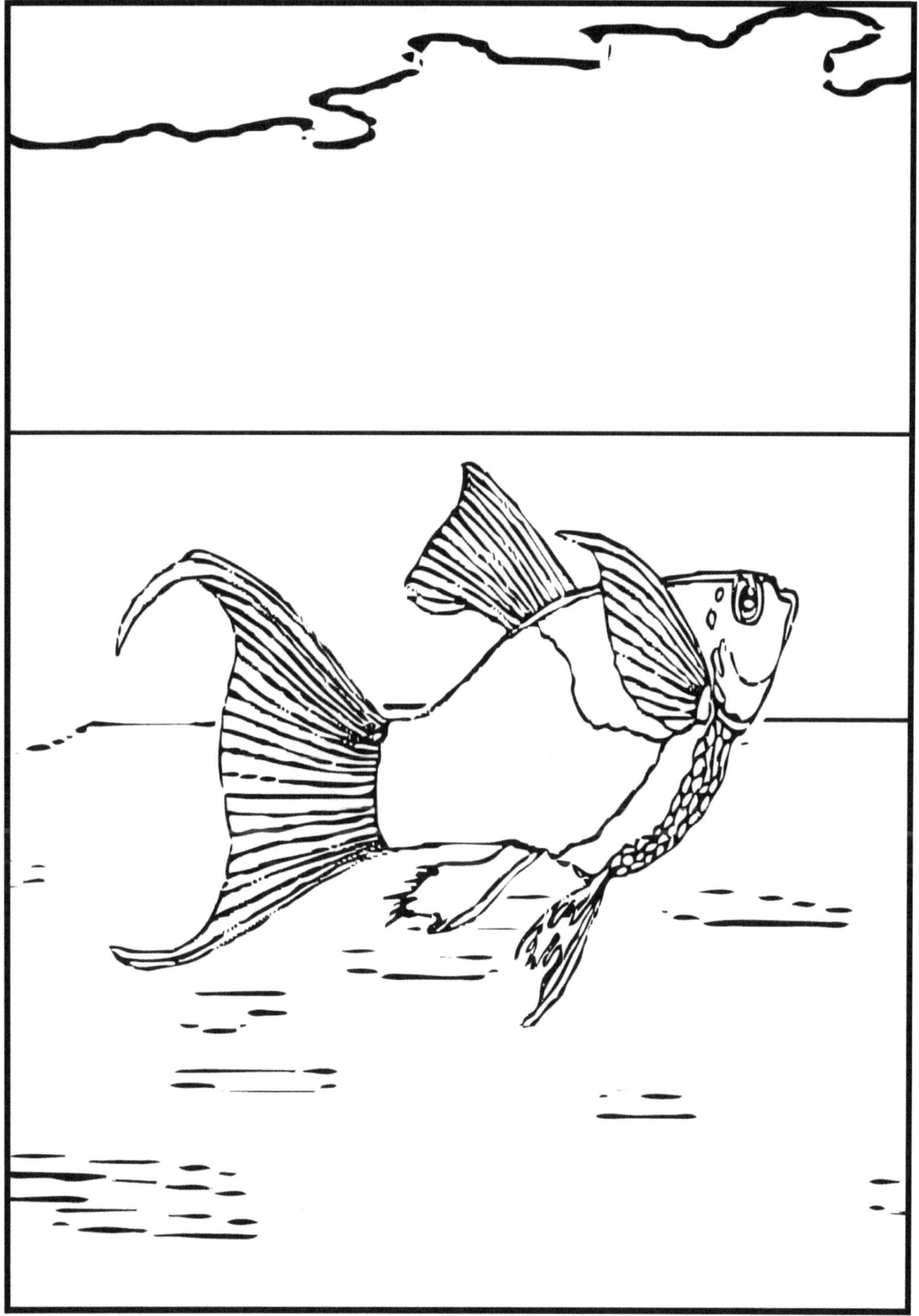

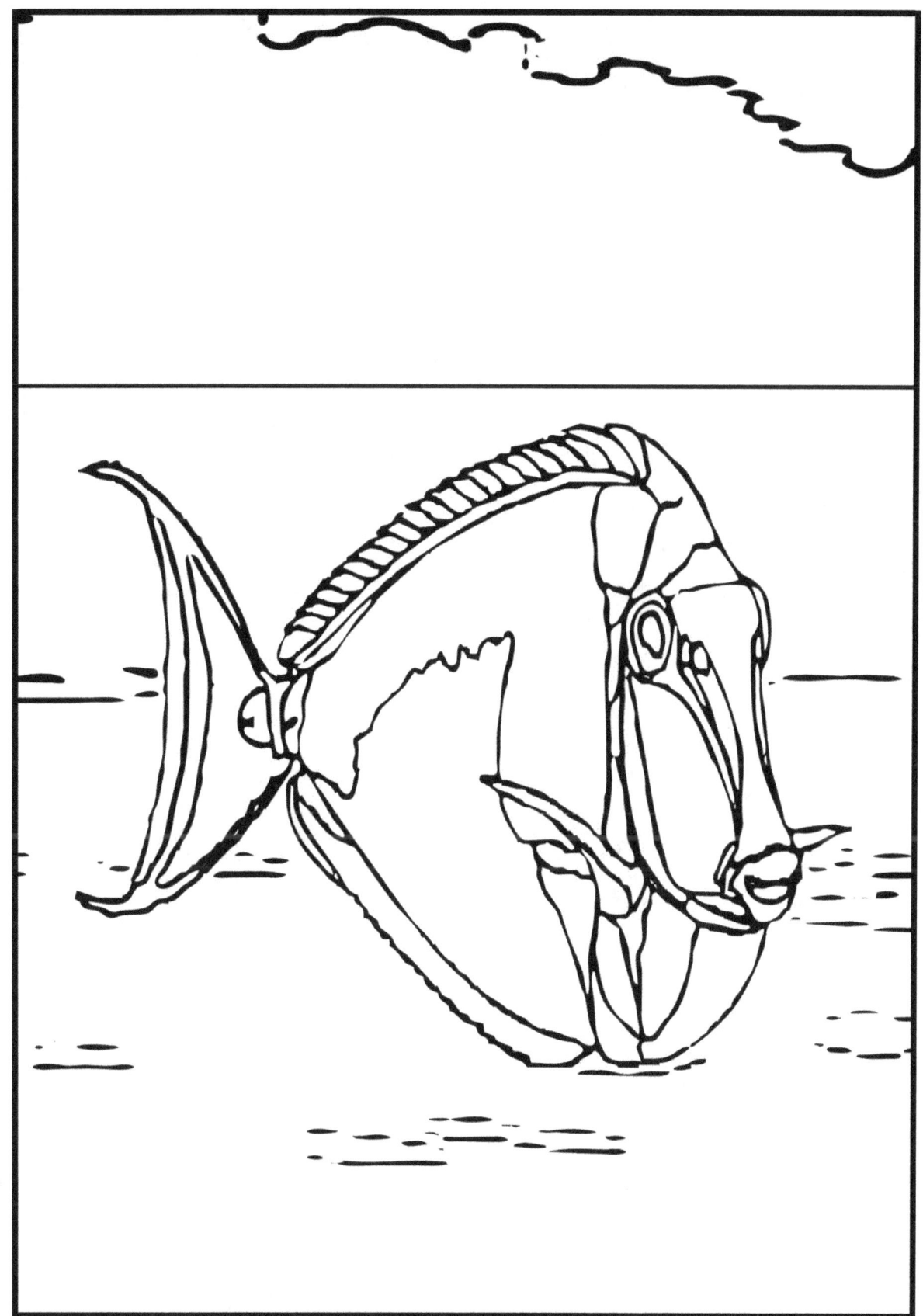

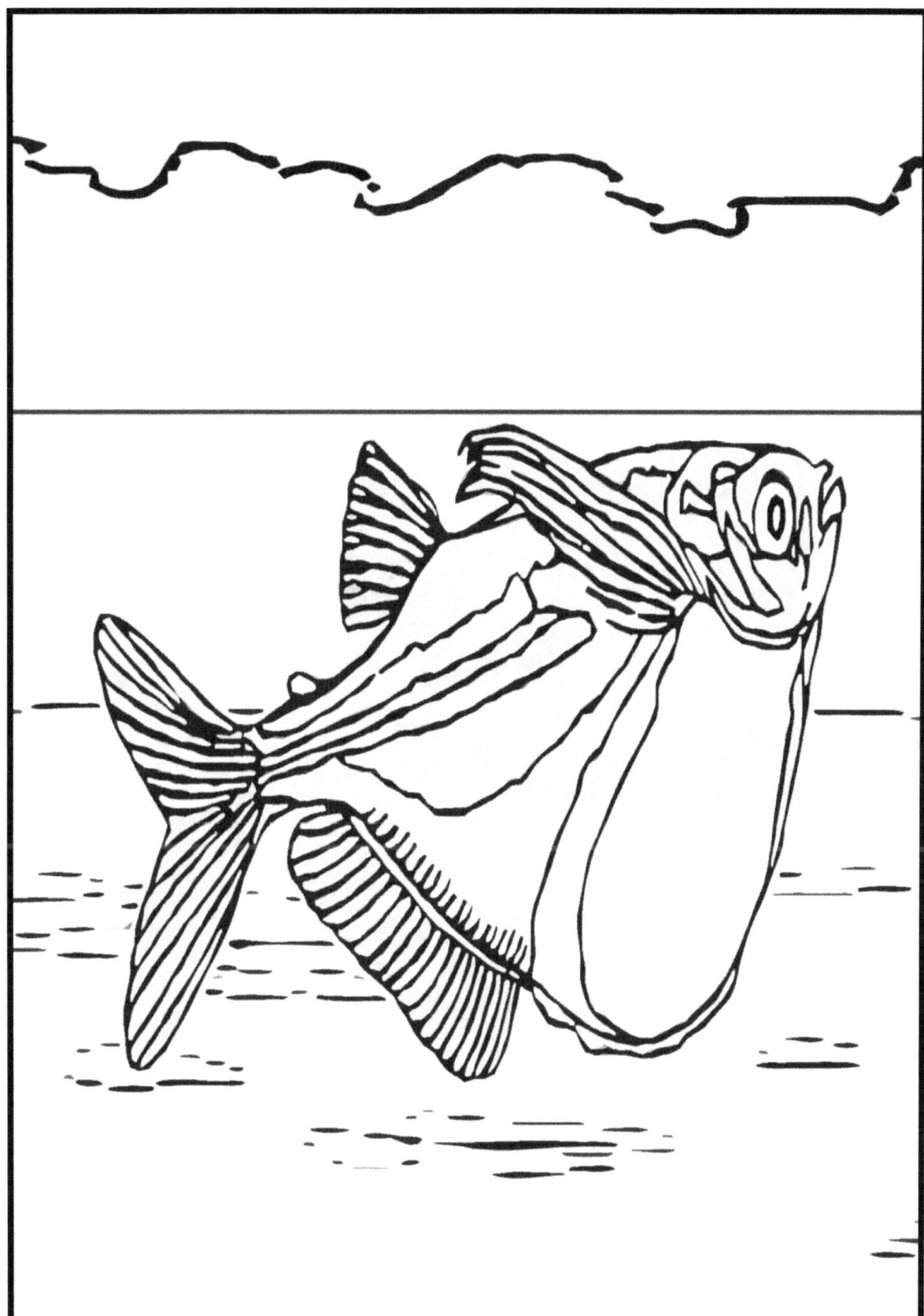

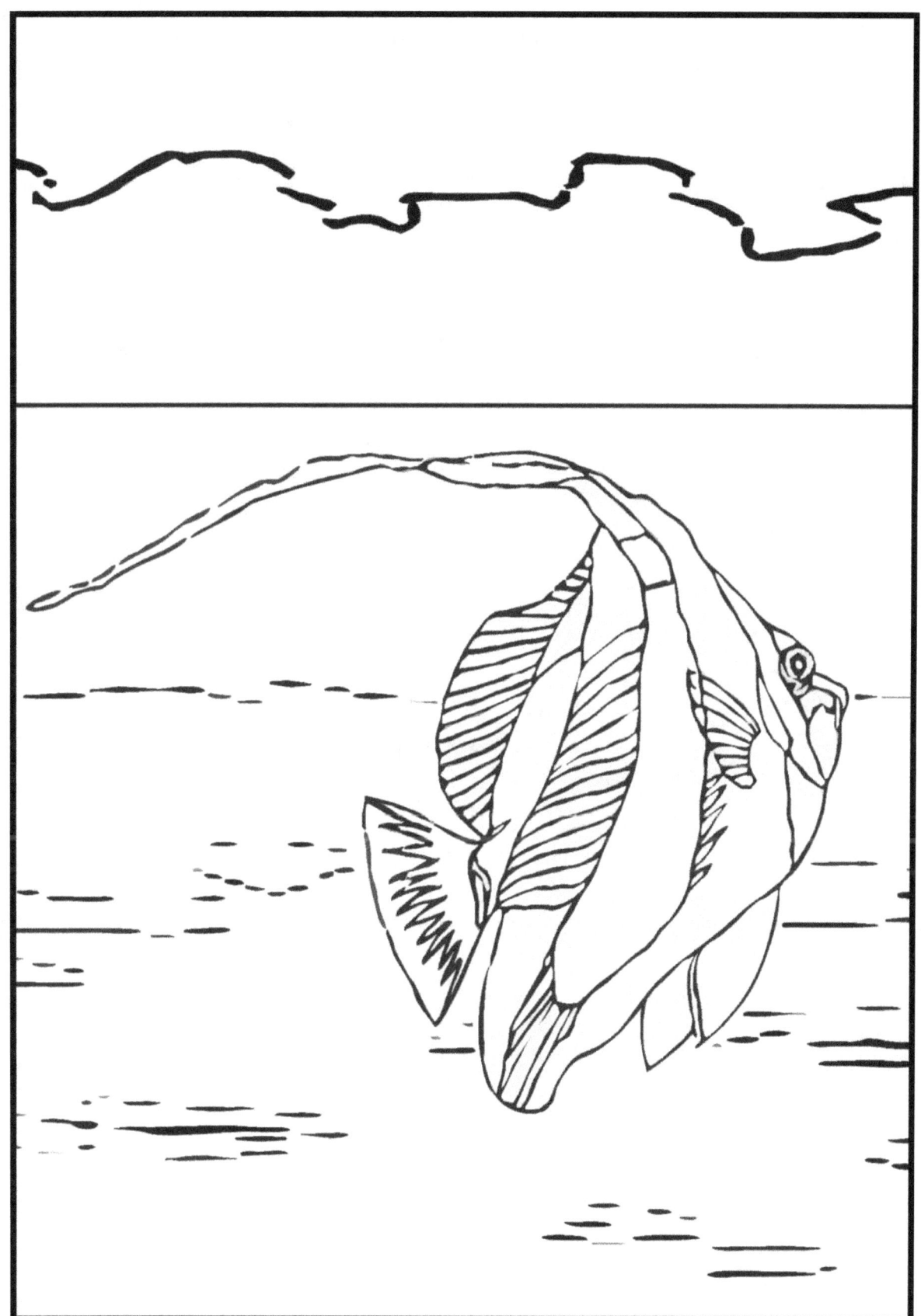

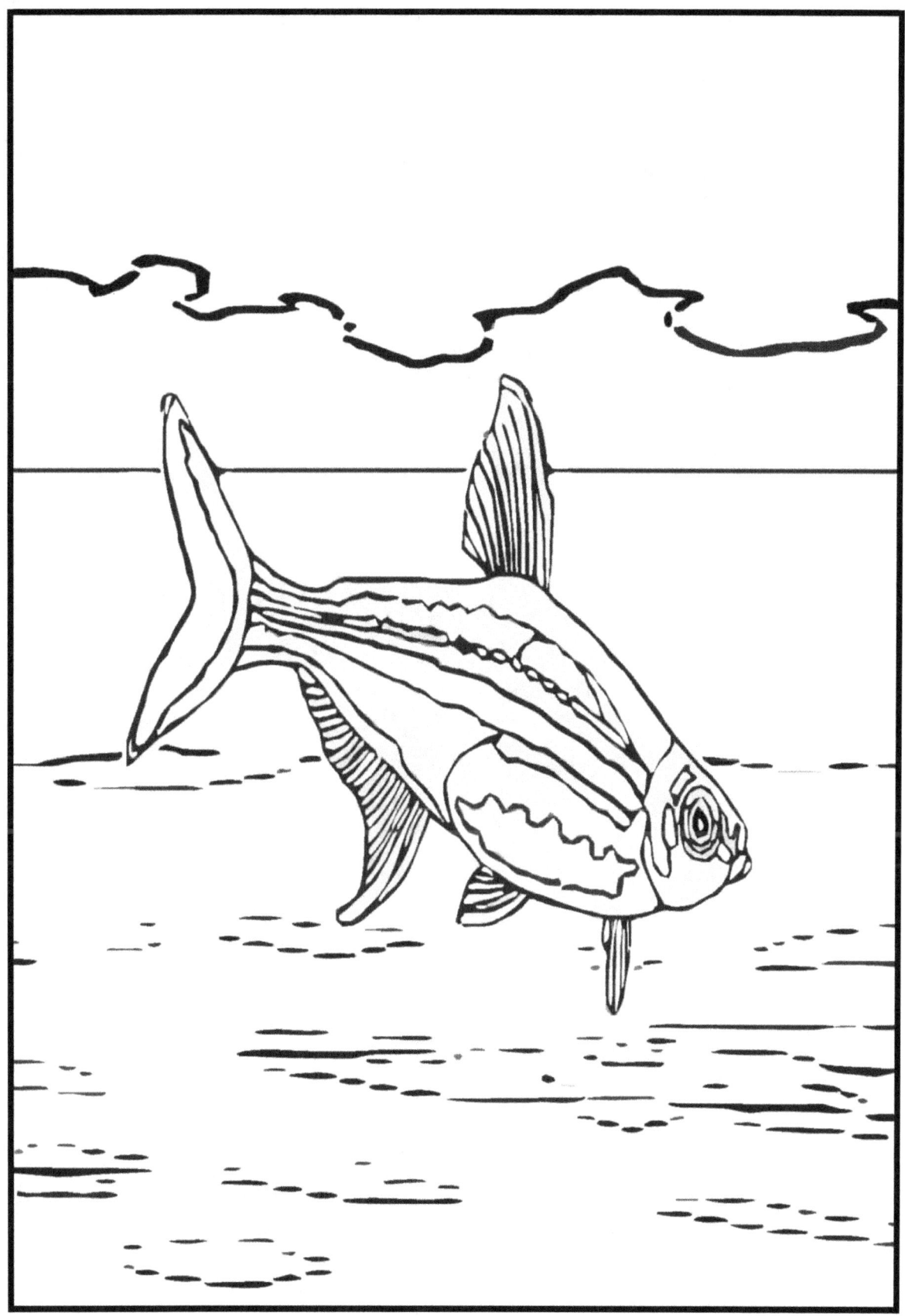

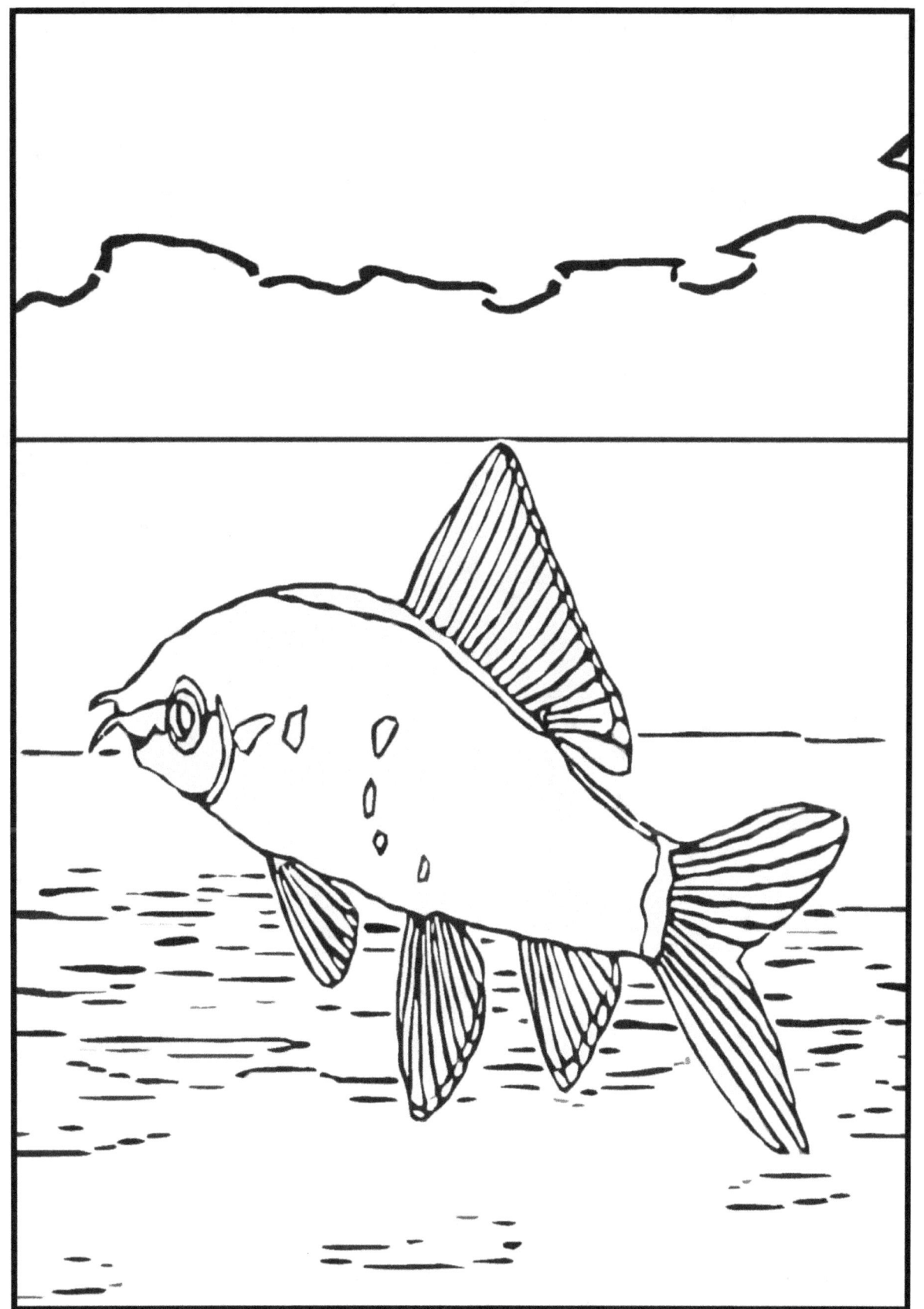

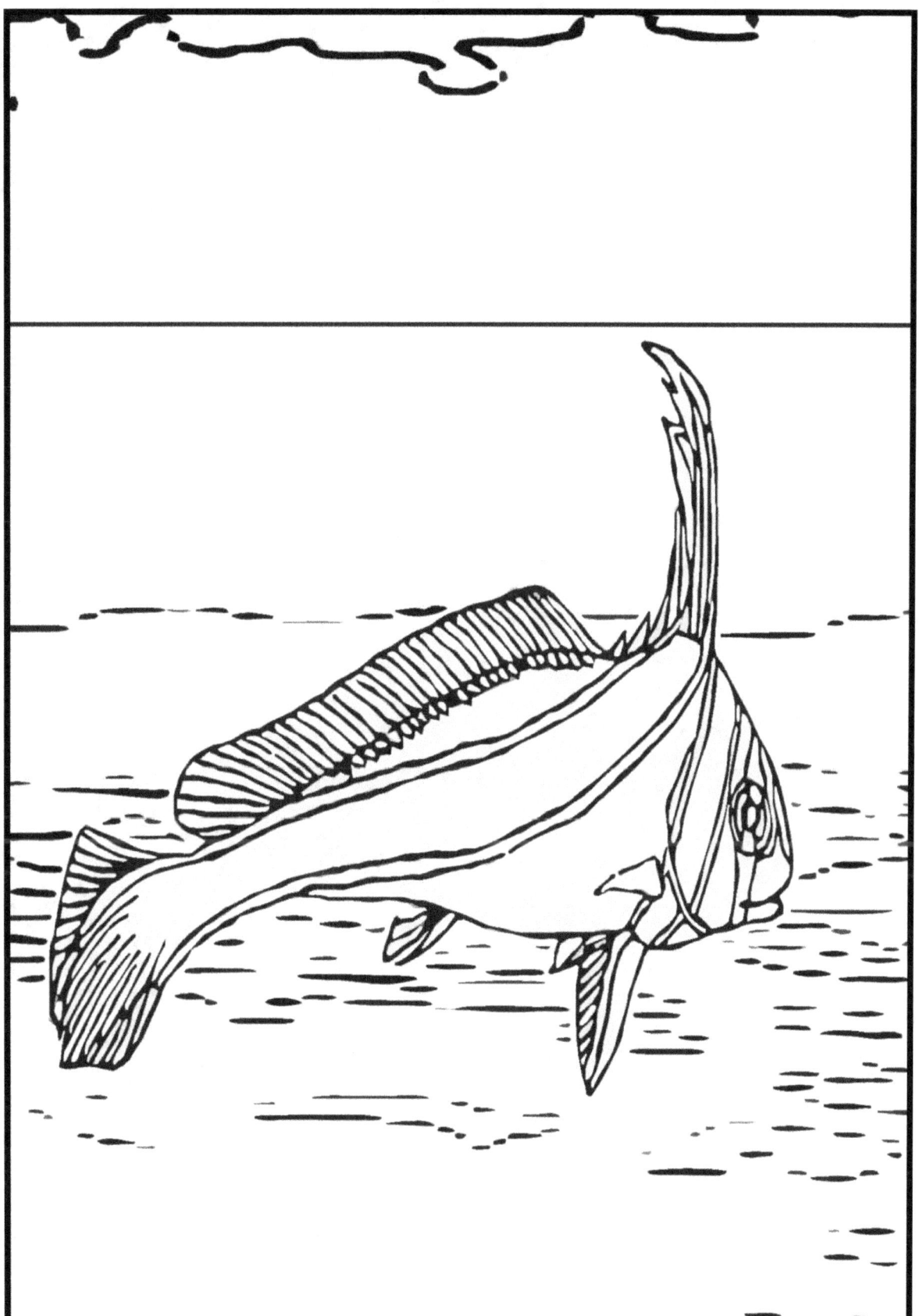

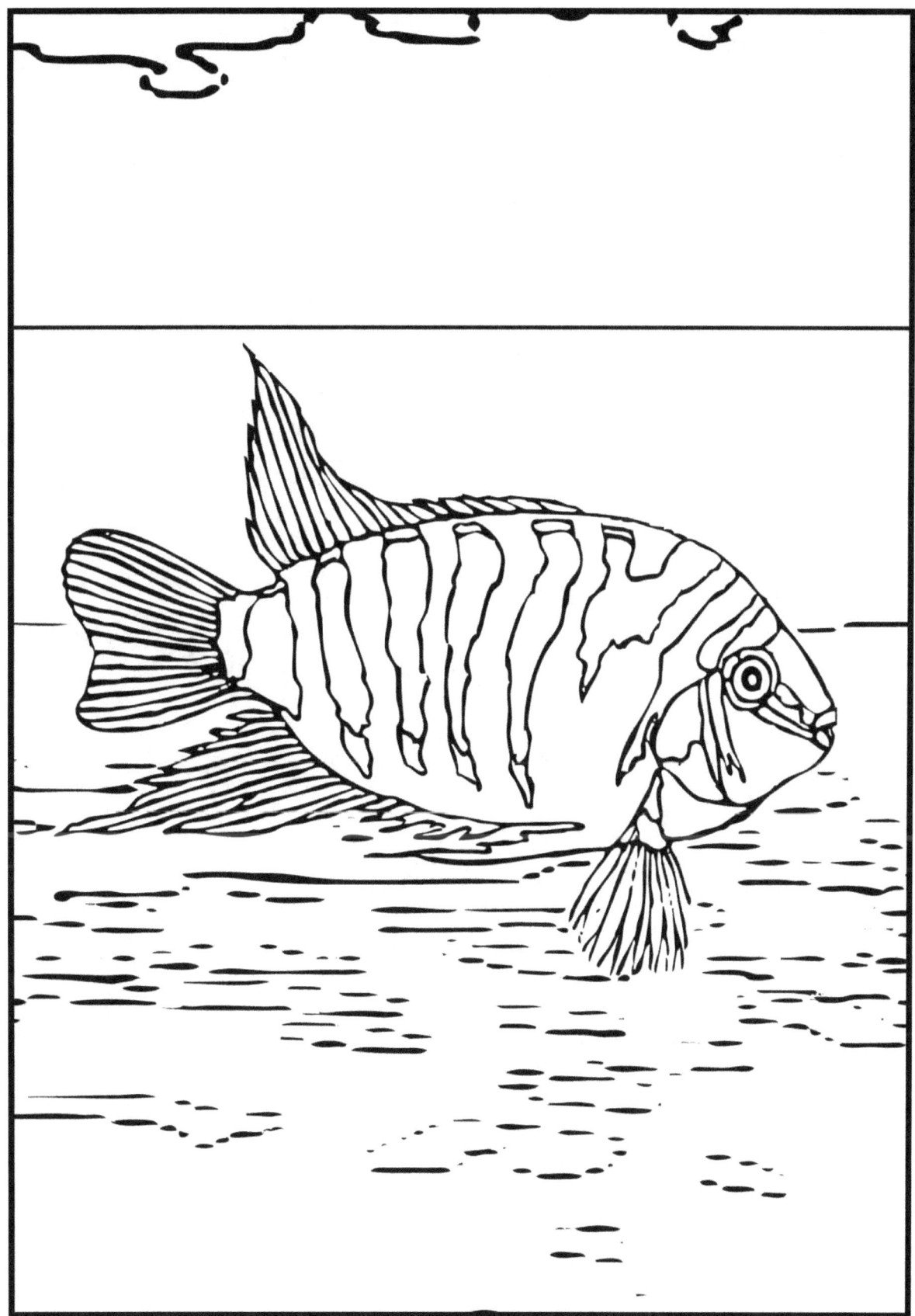

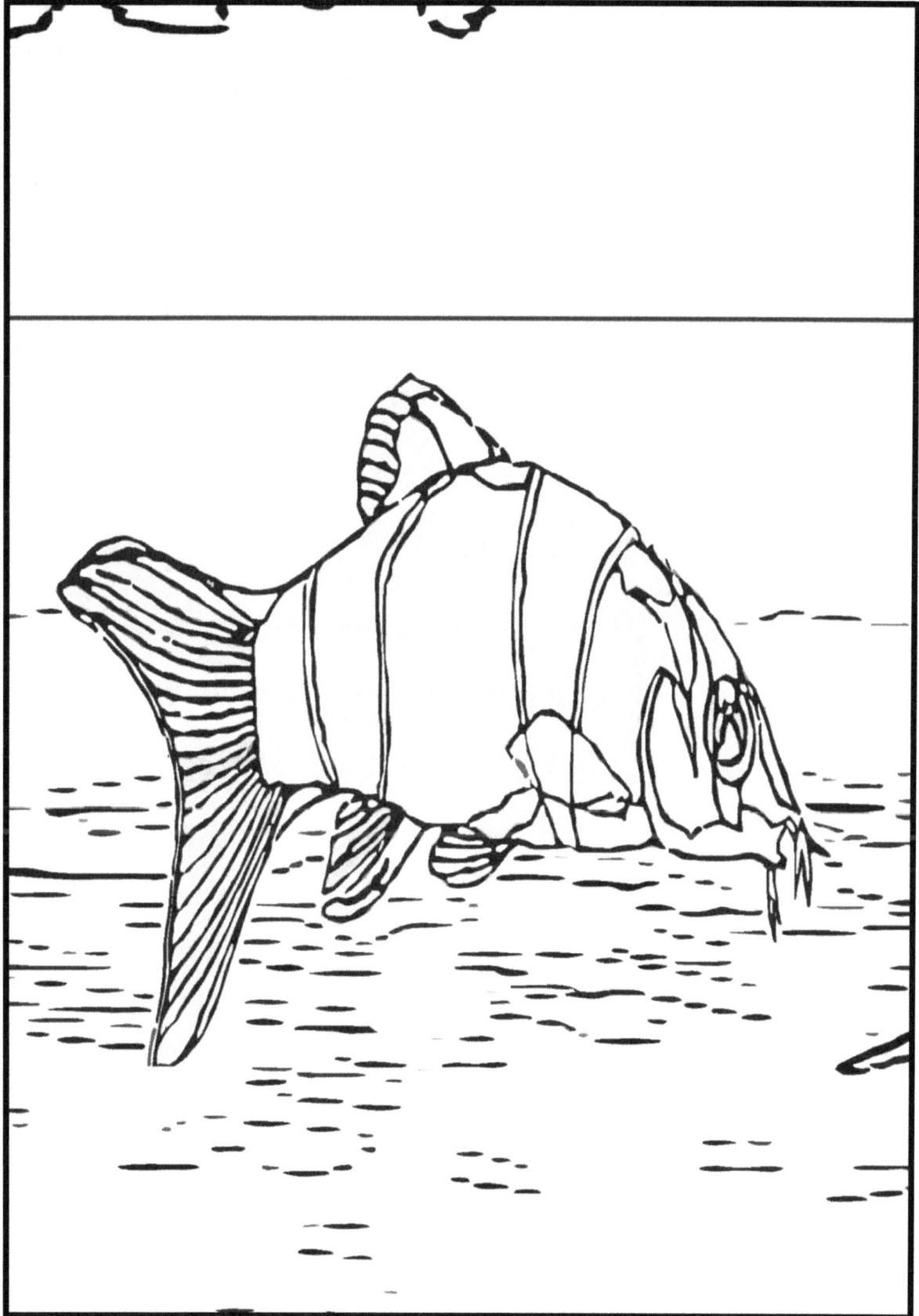

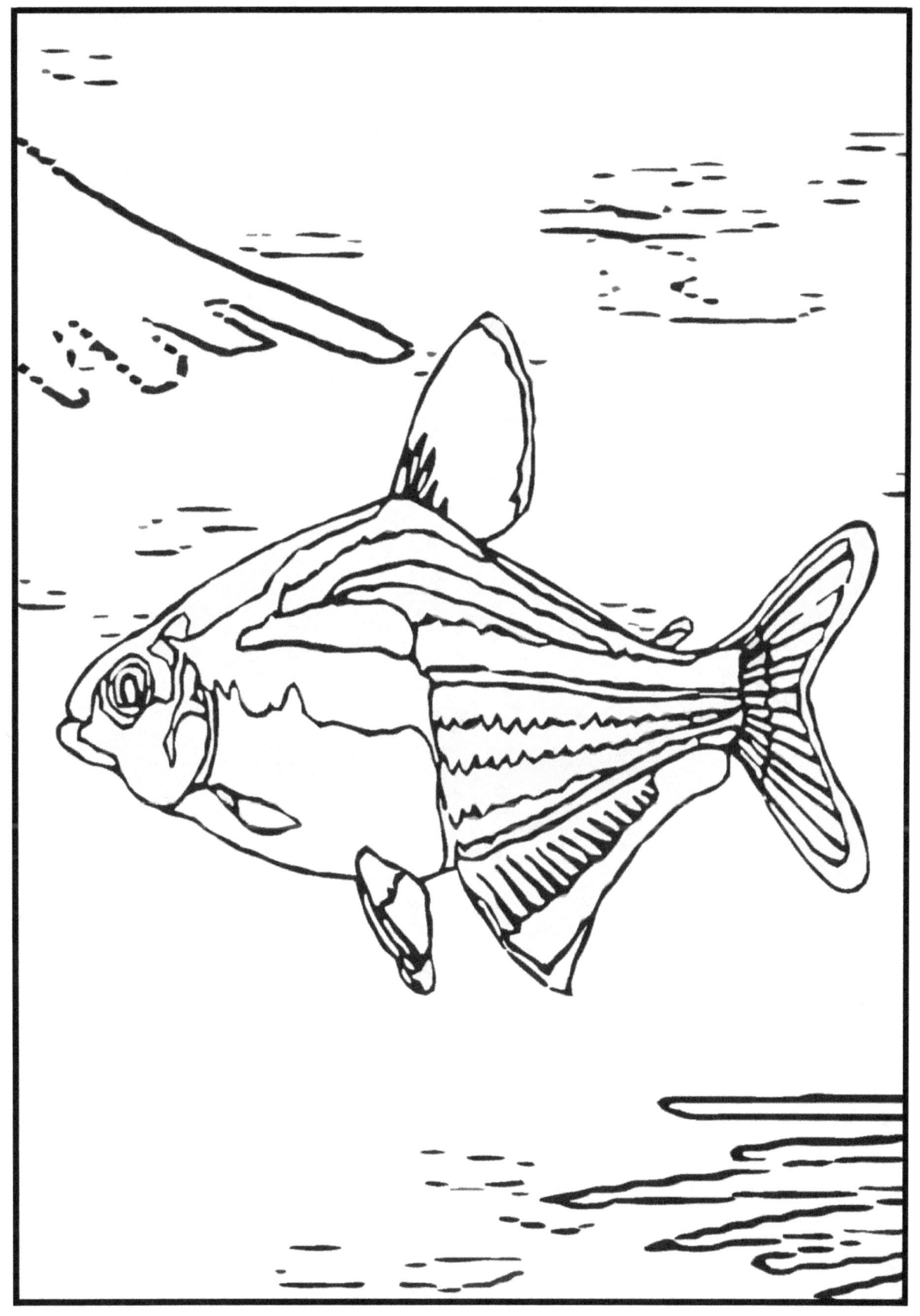

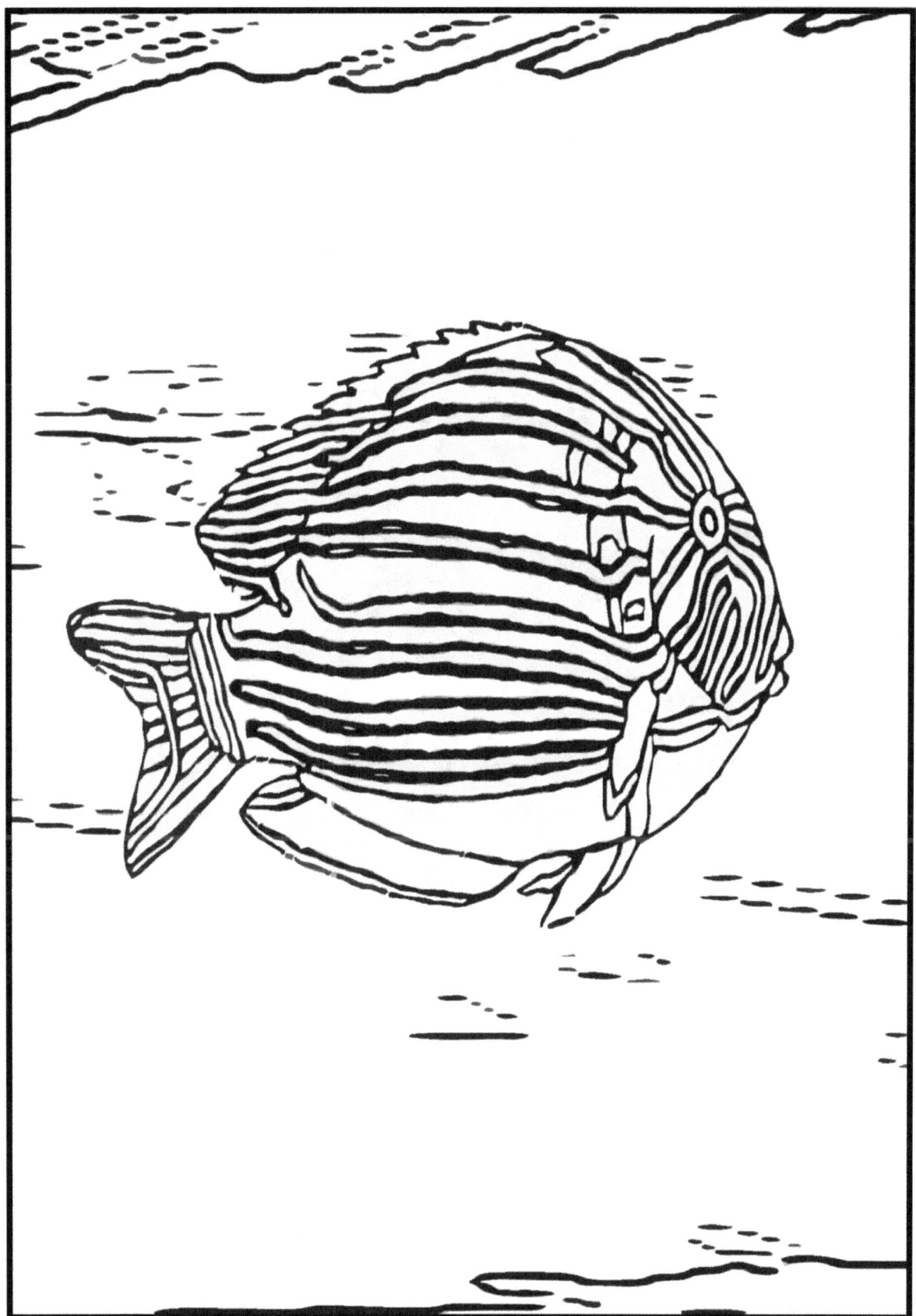

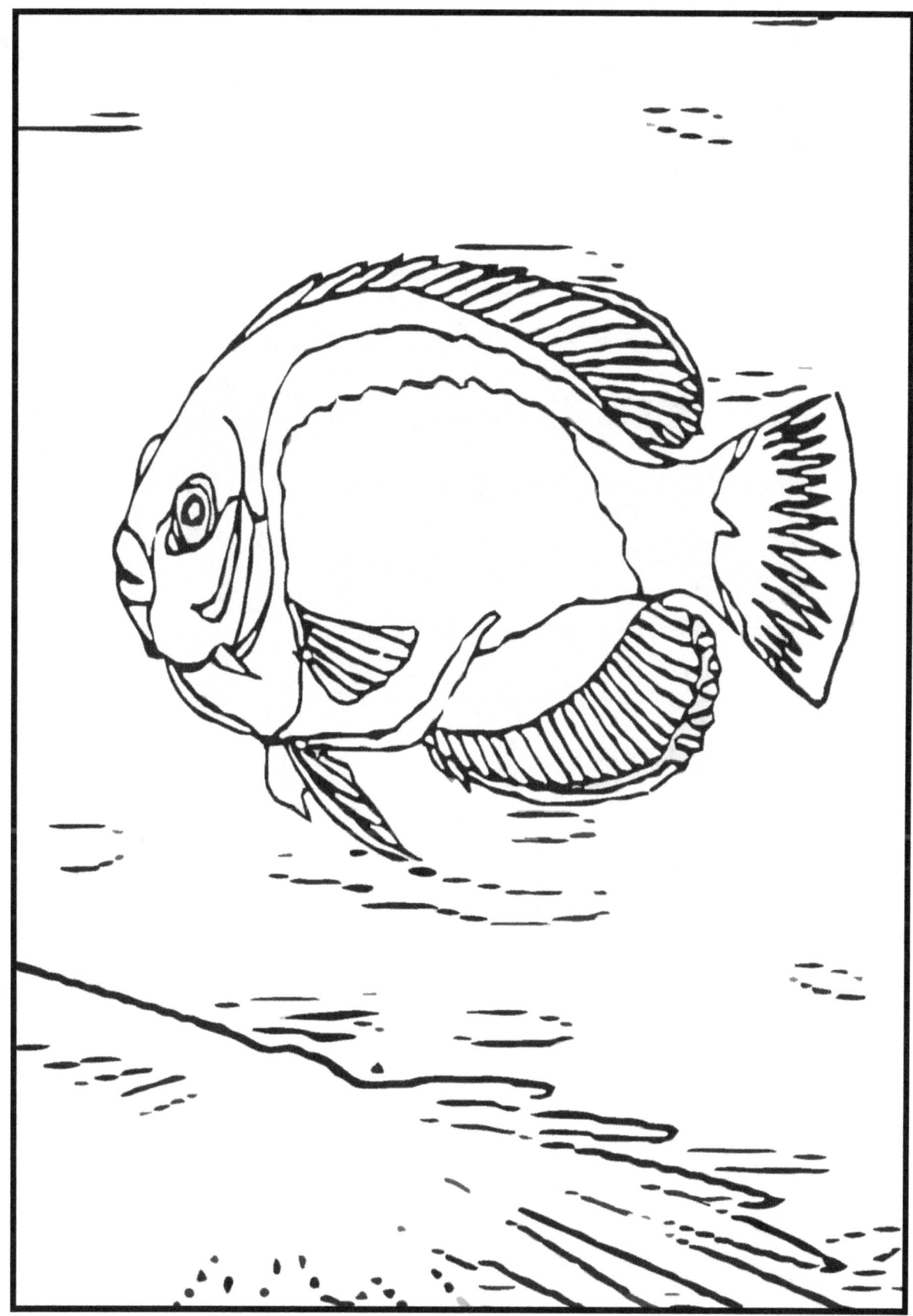

REPTILES!

Coloring Book

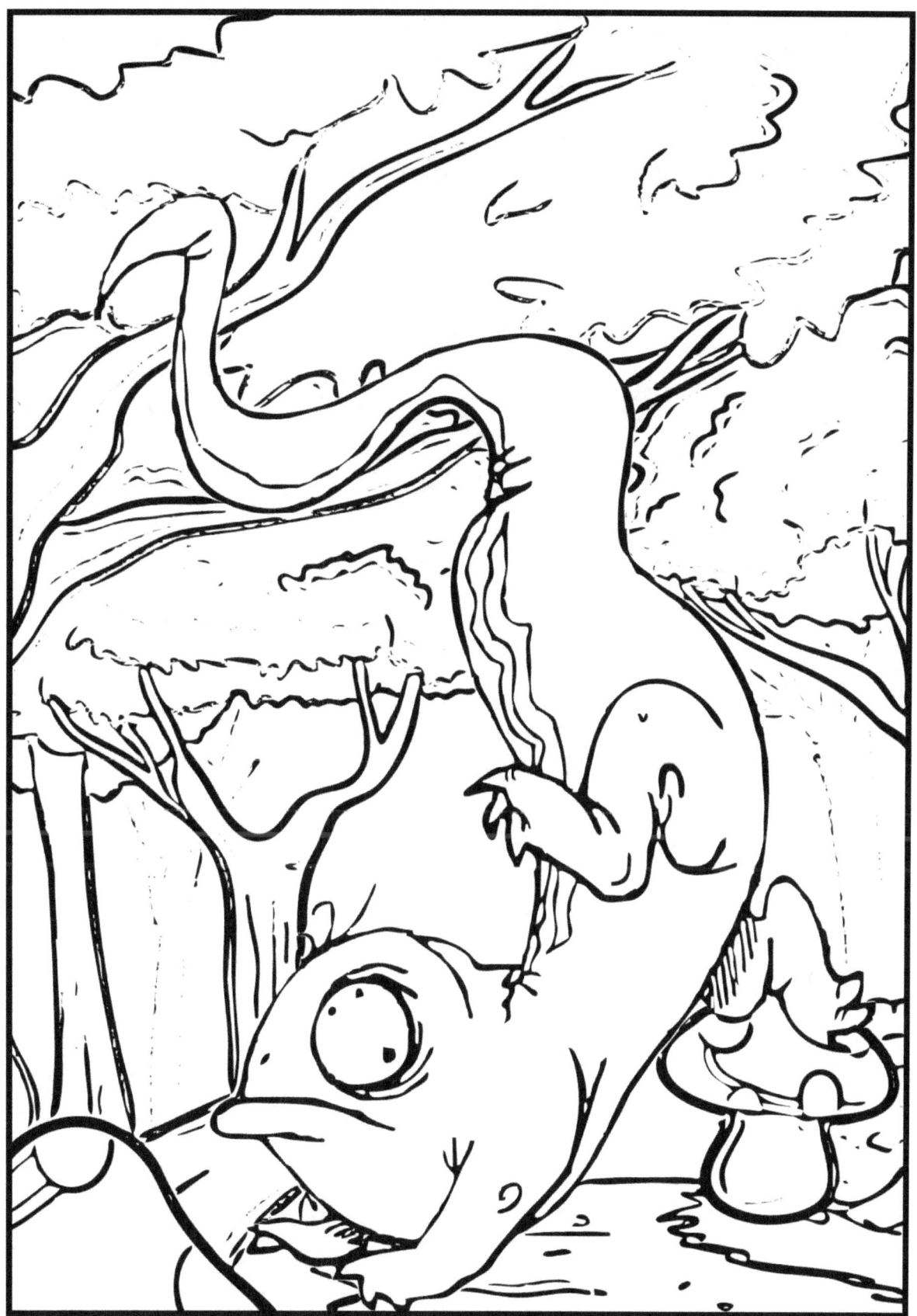

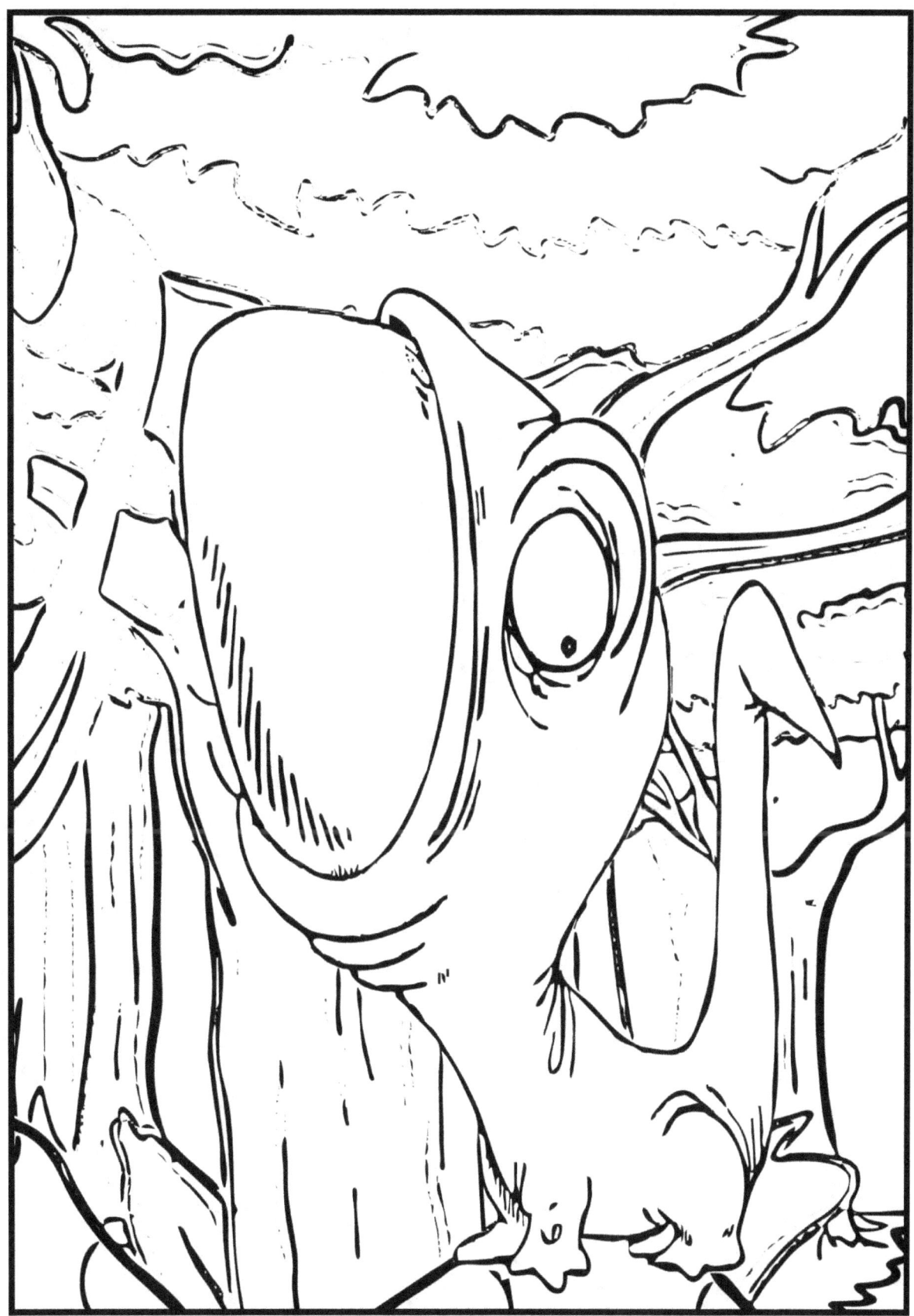

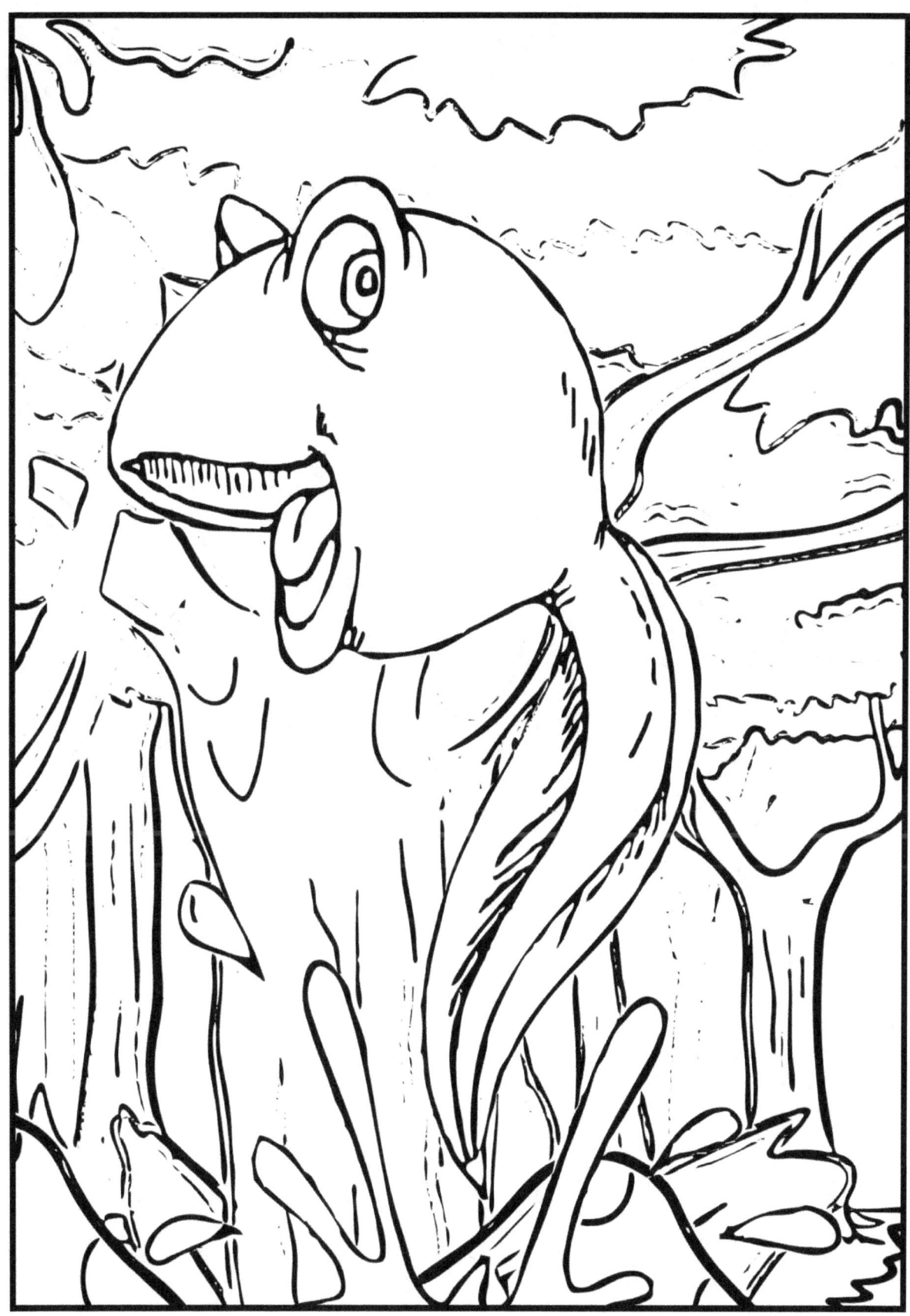

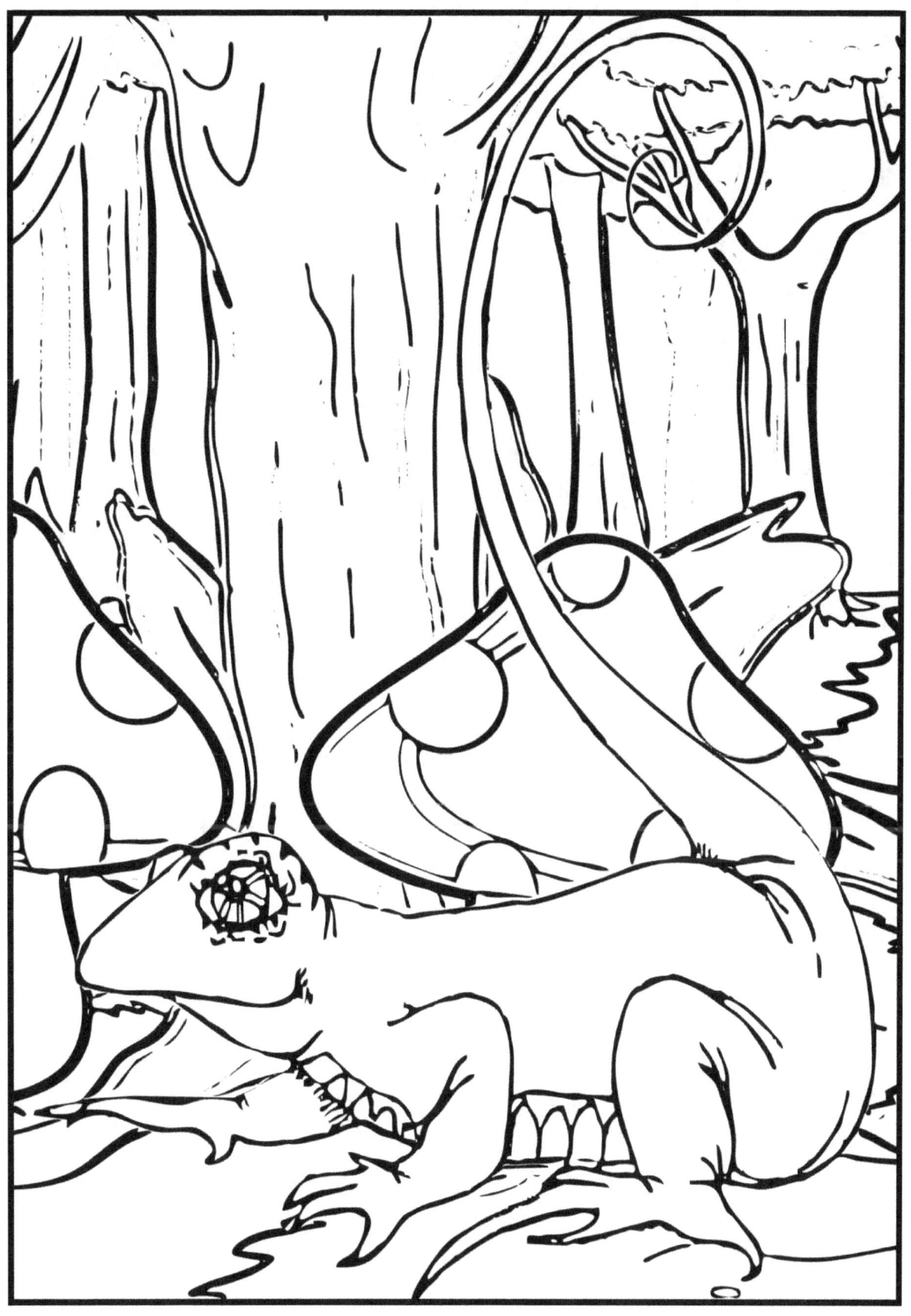

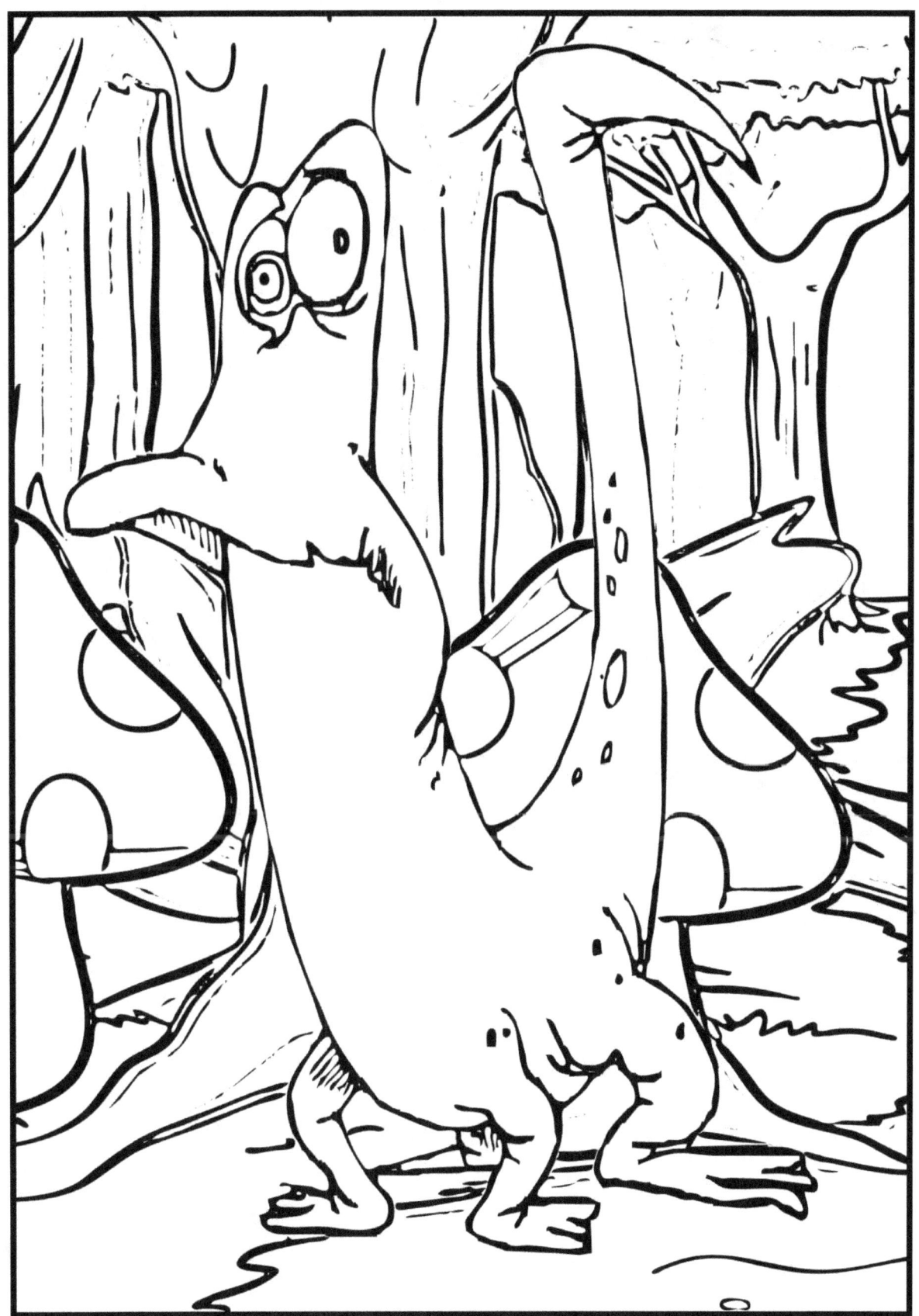

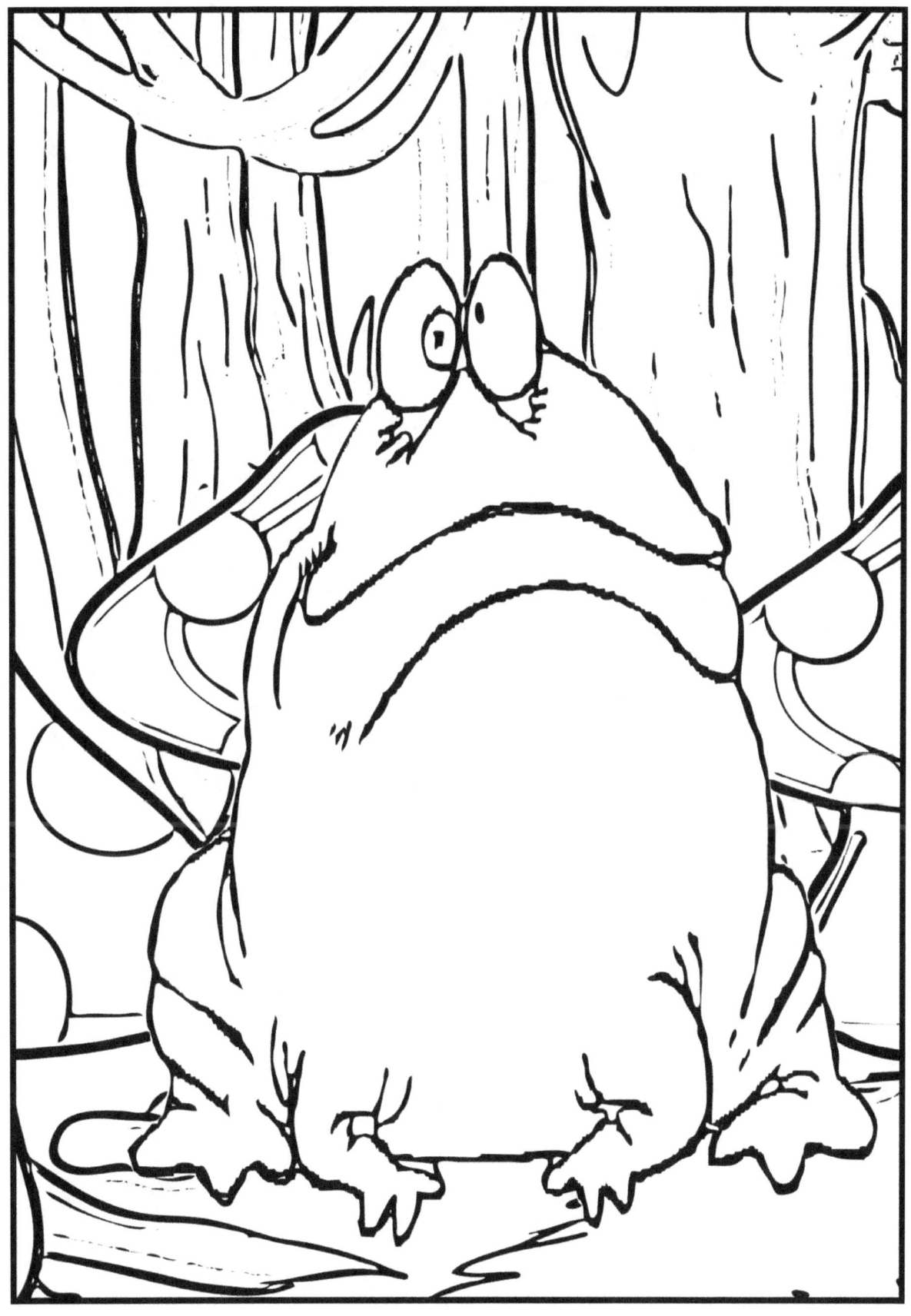

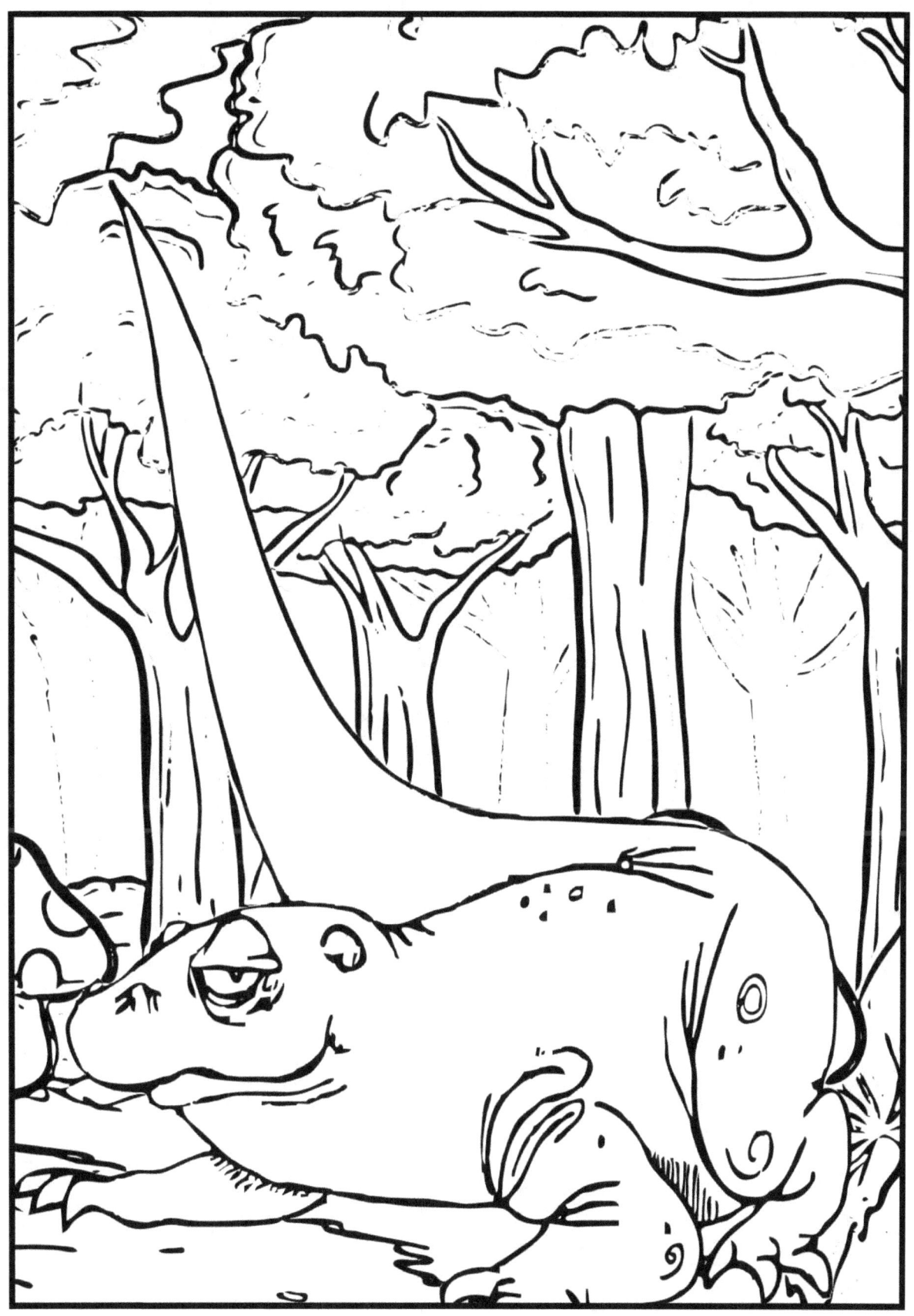

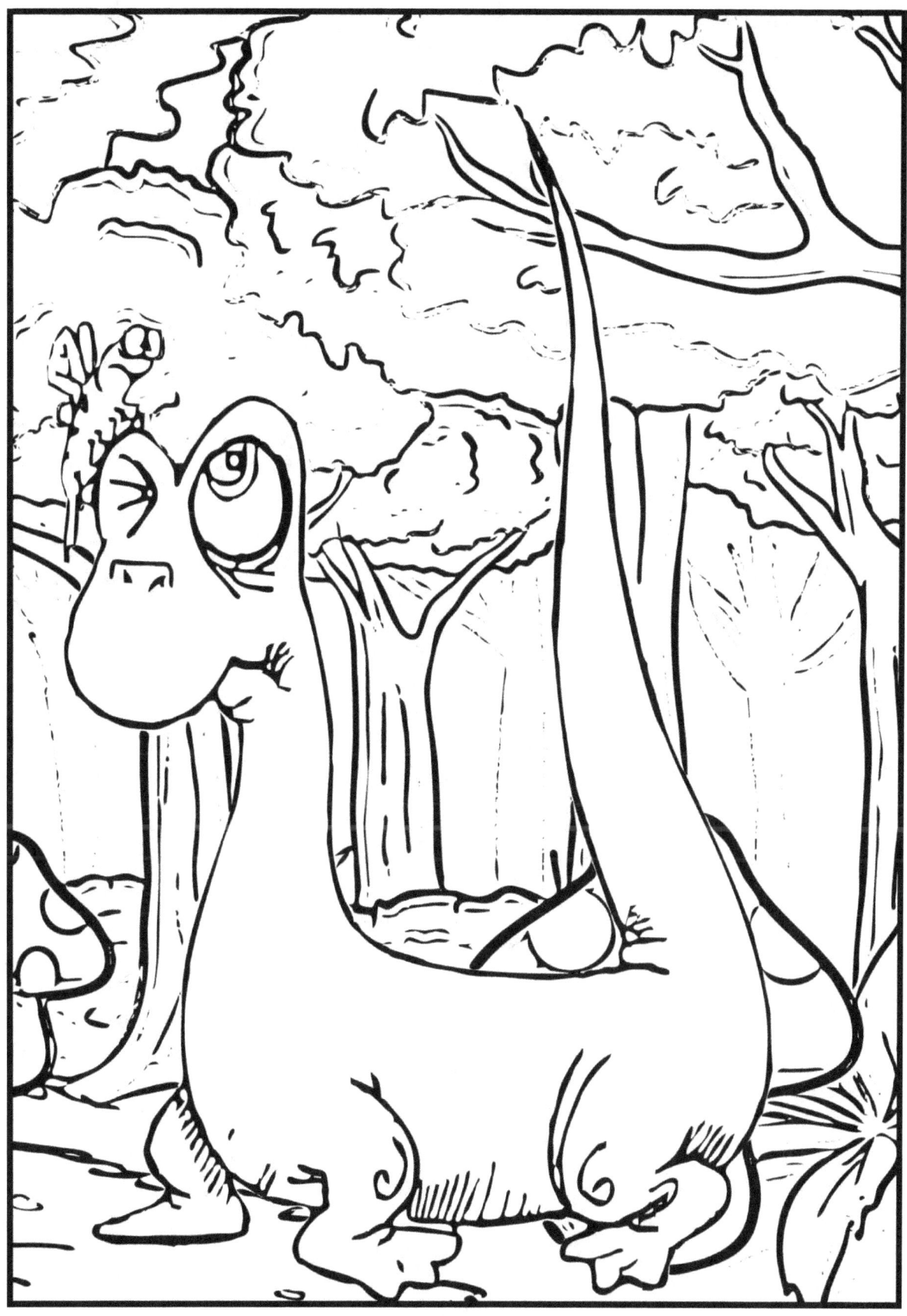

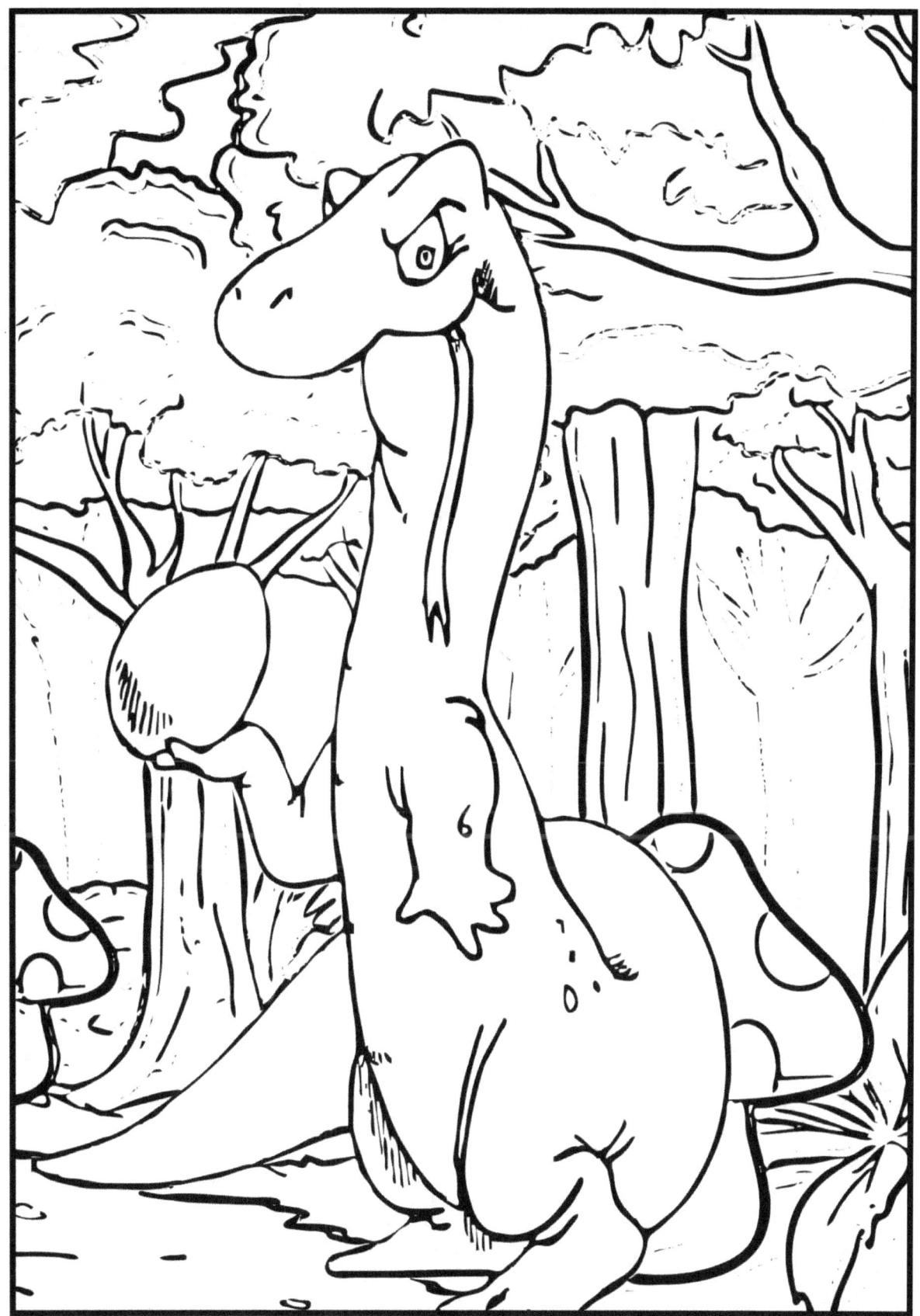

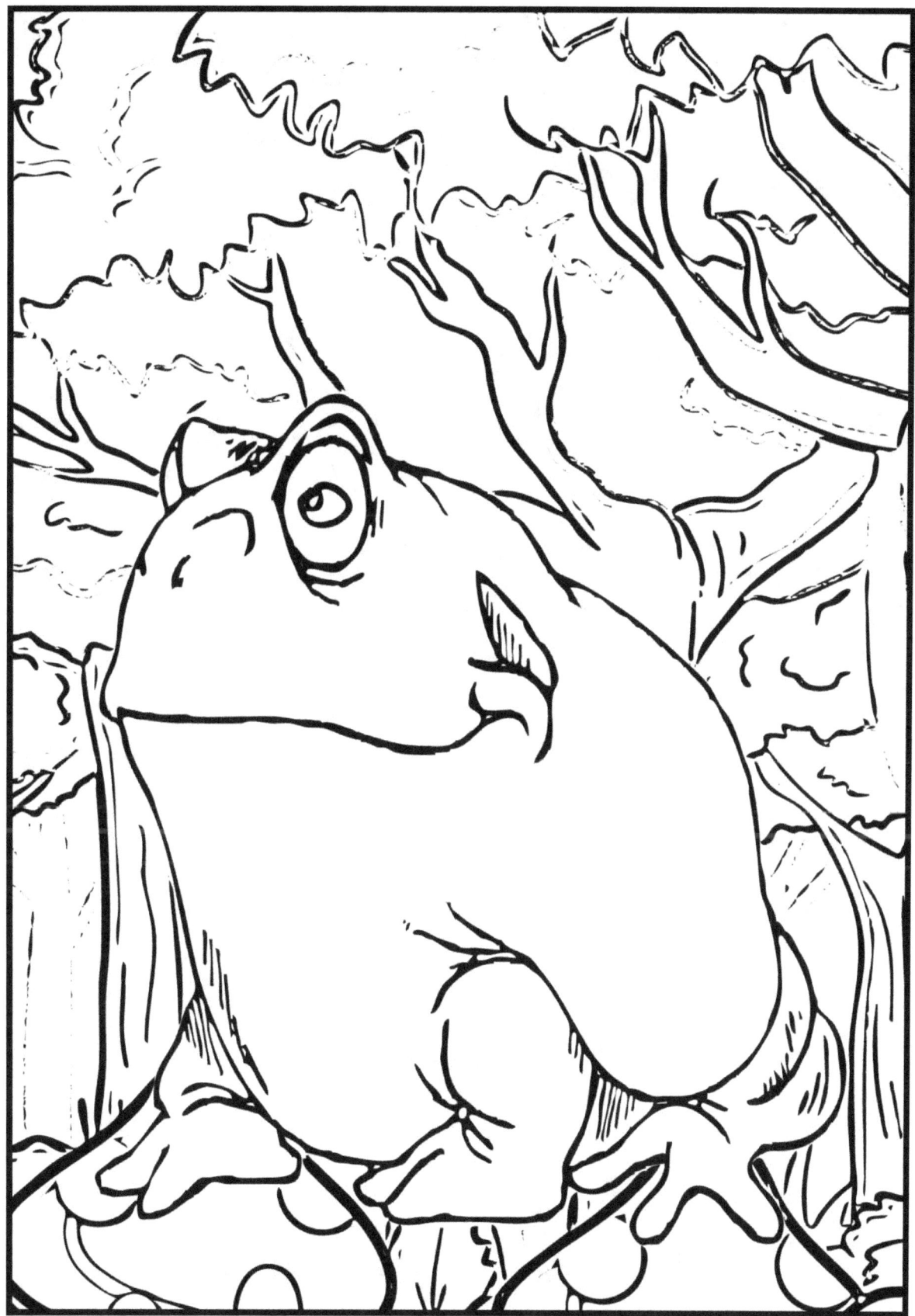

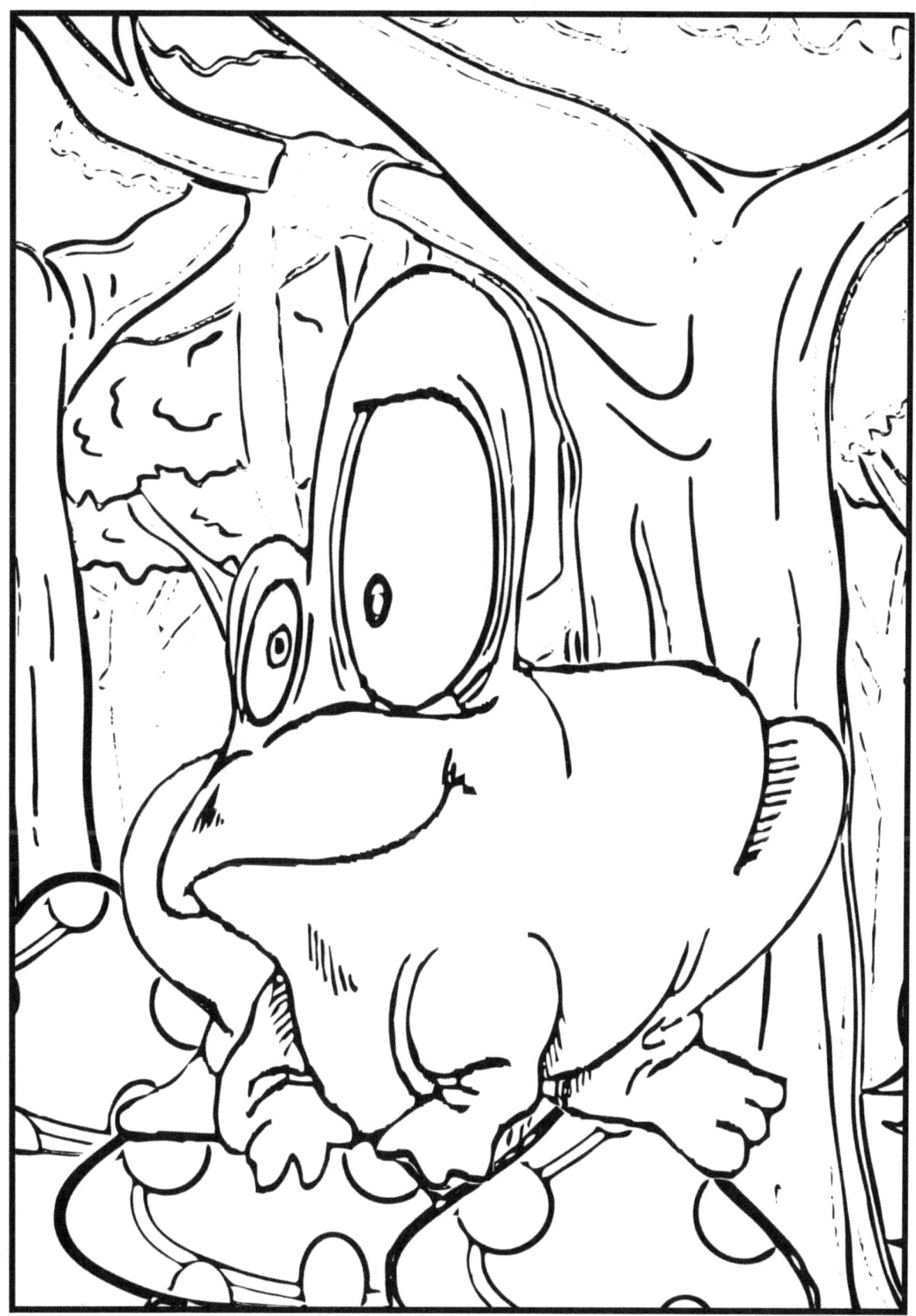

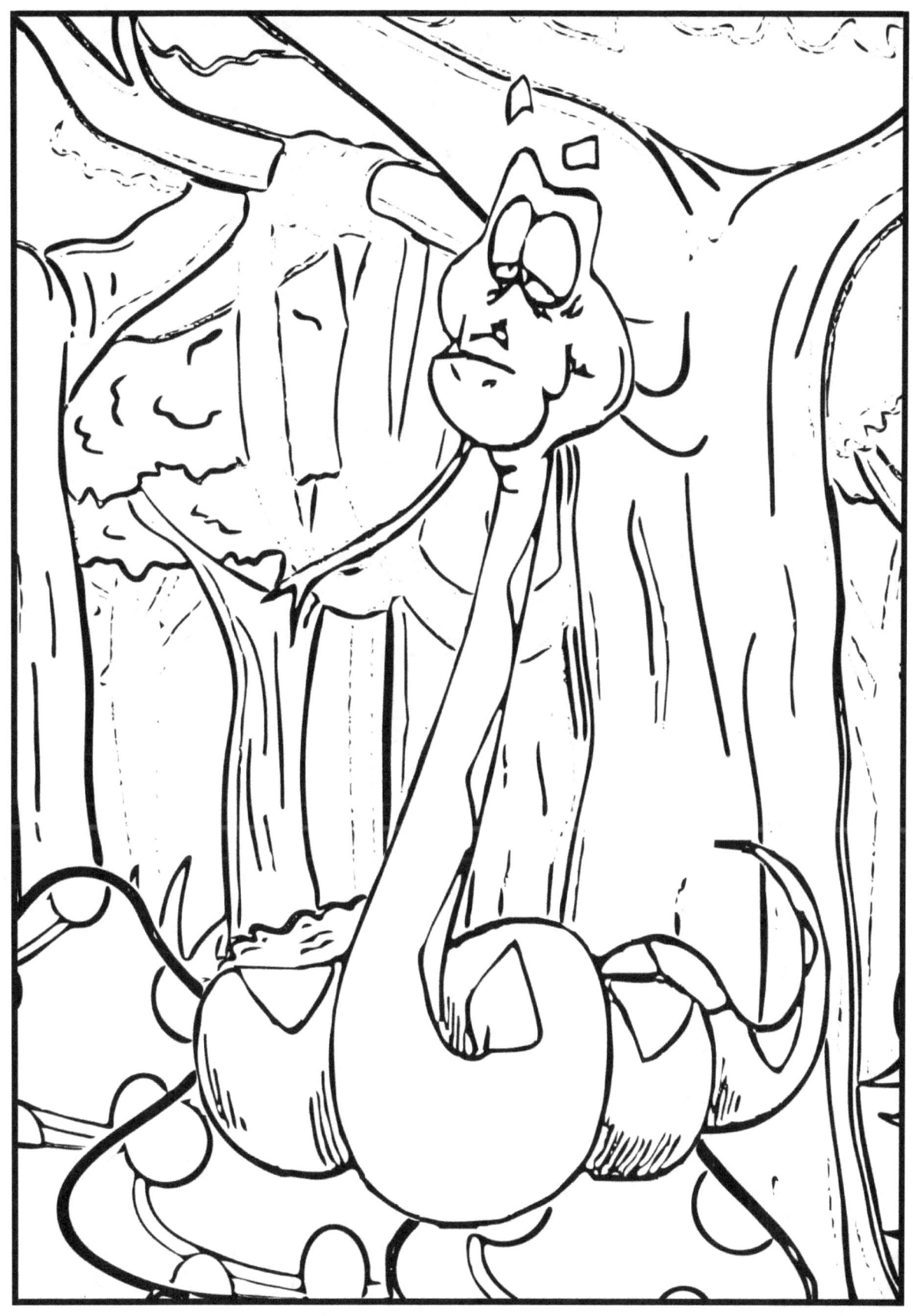

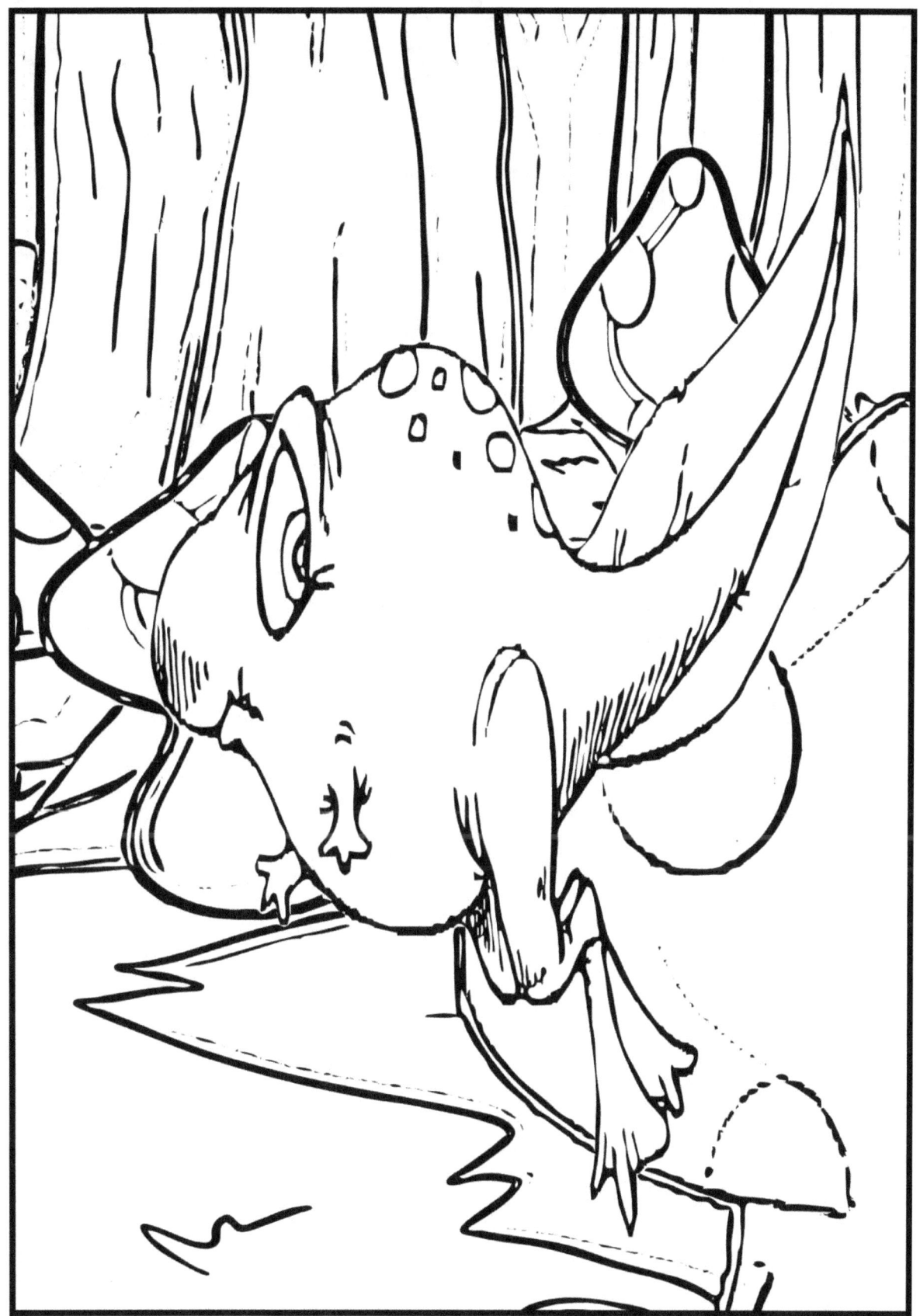

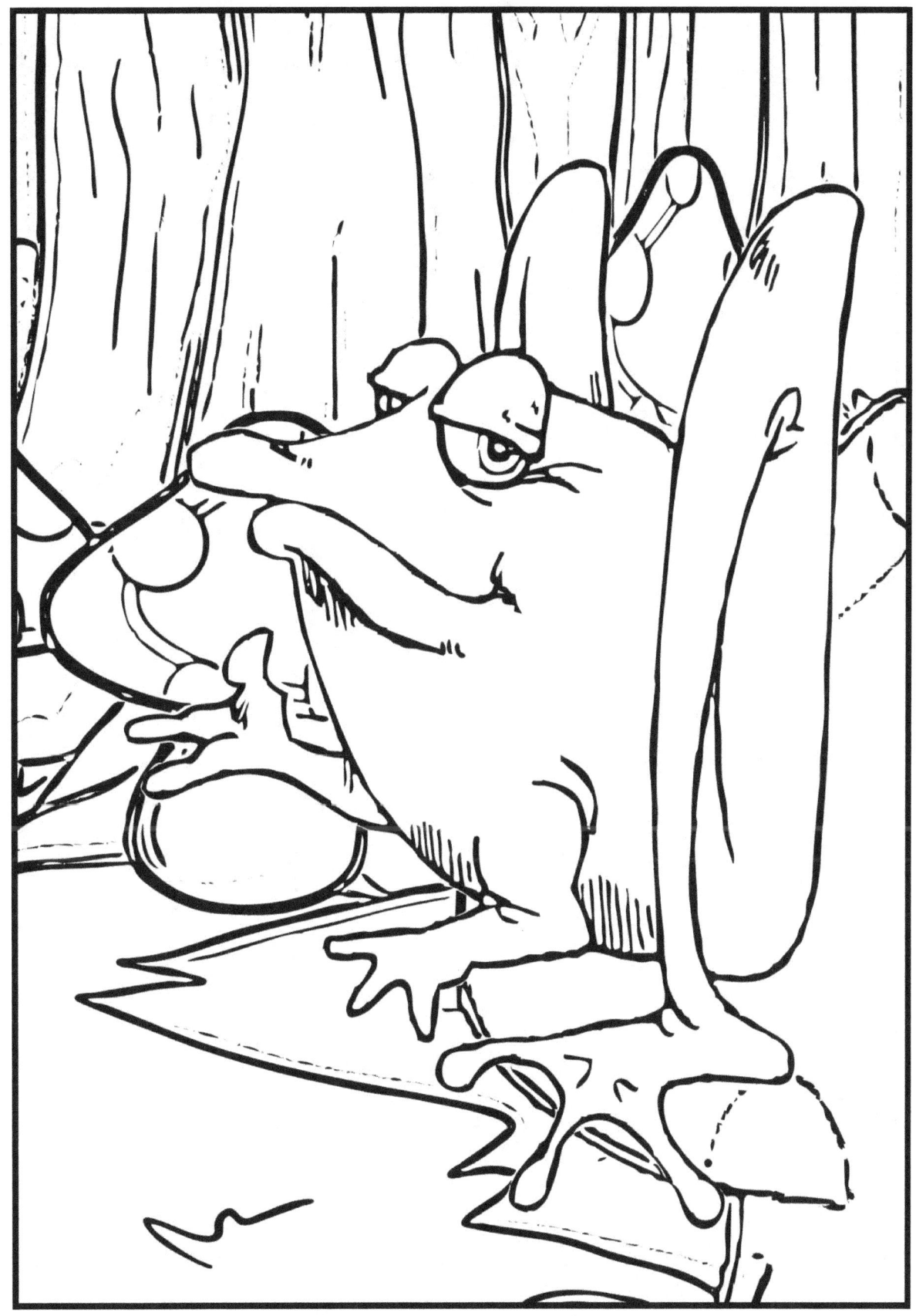

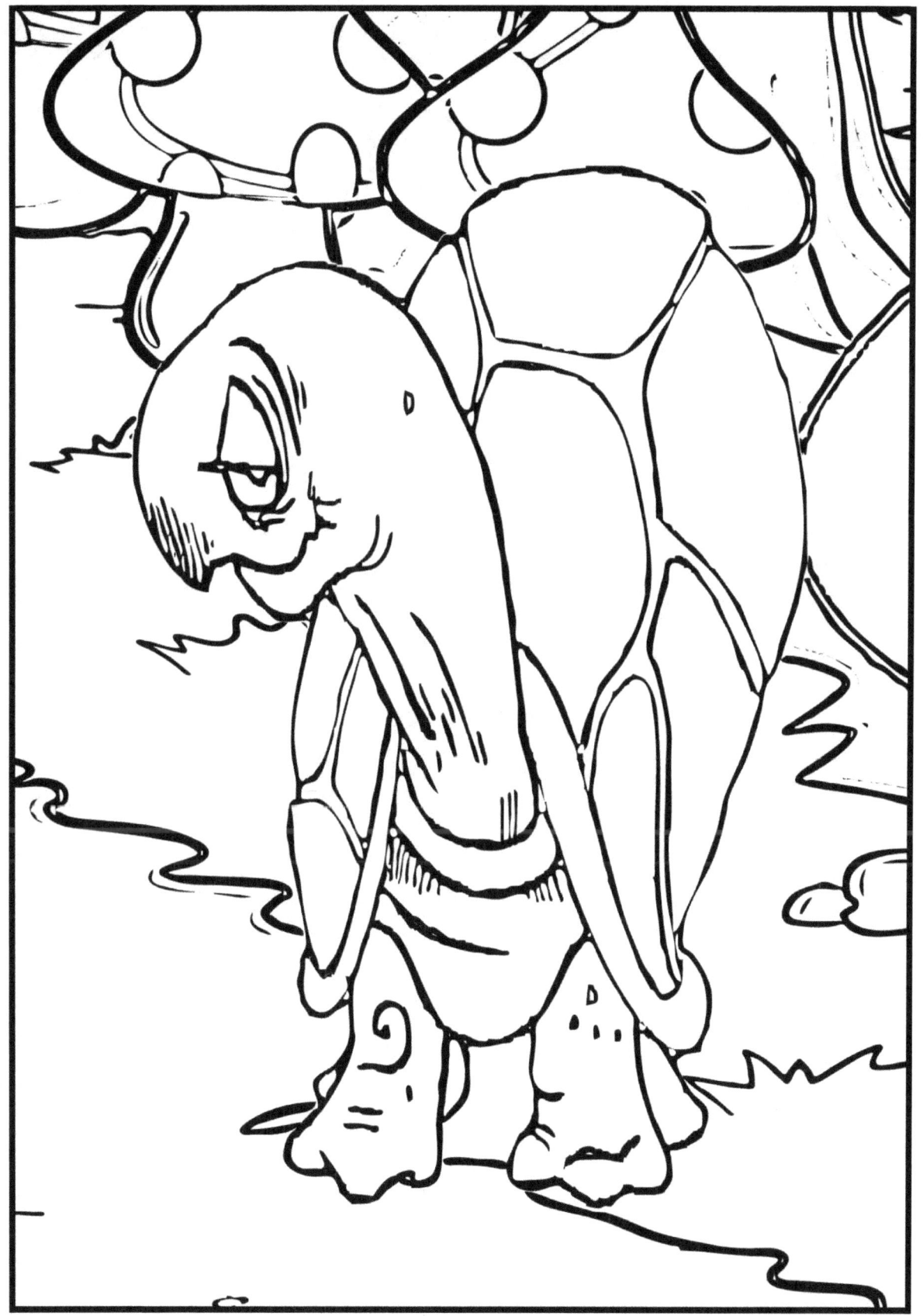

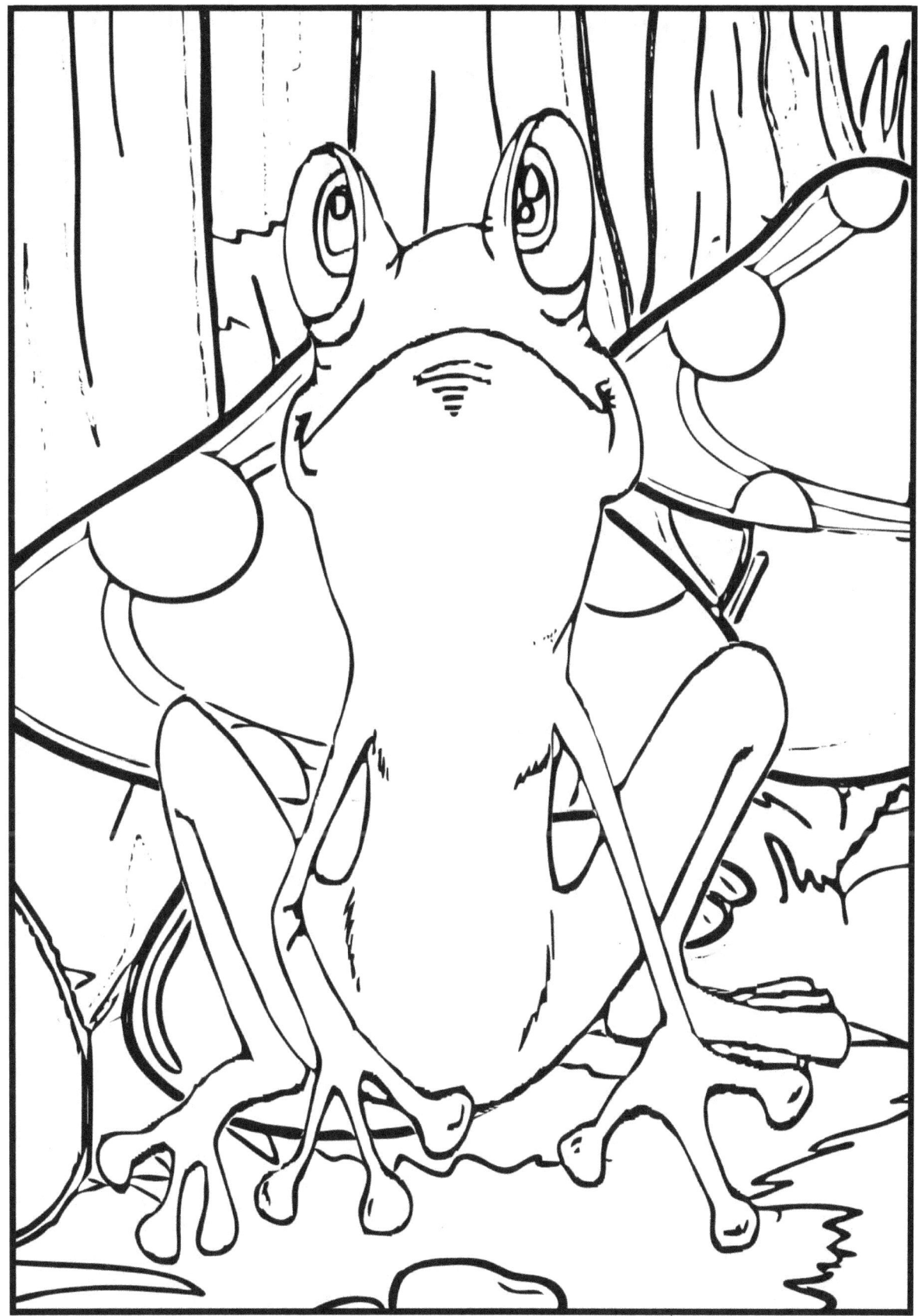

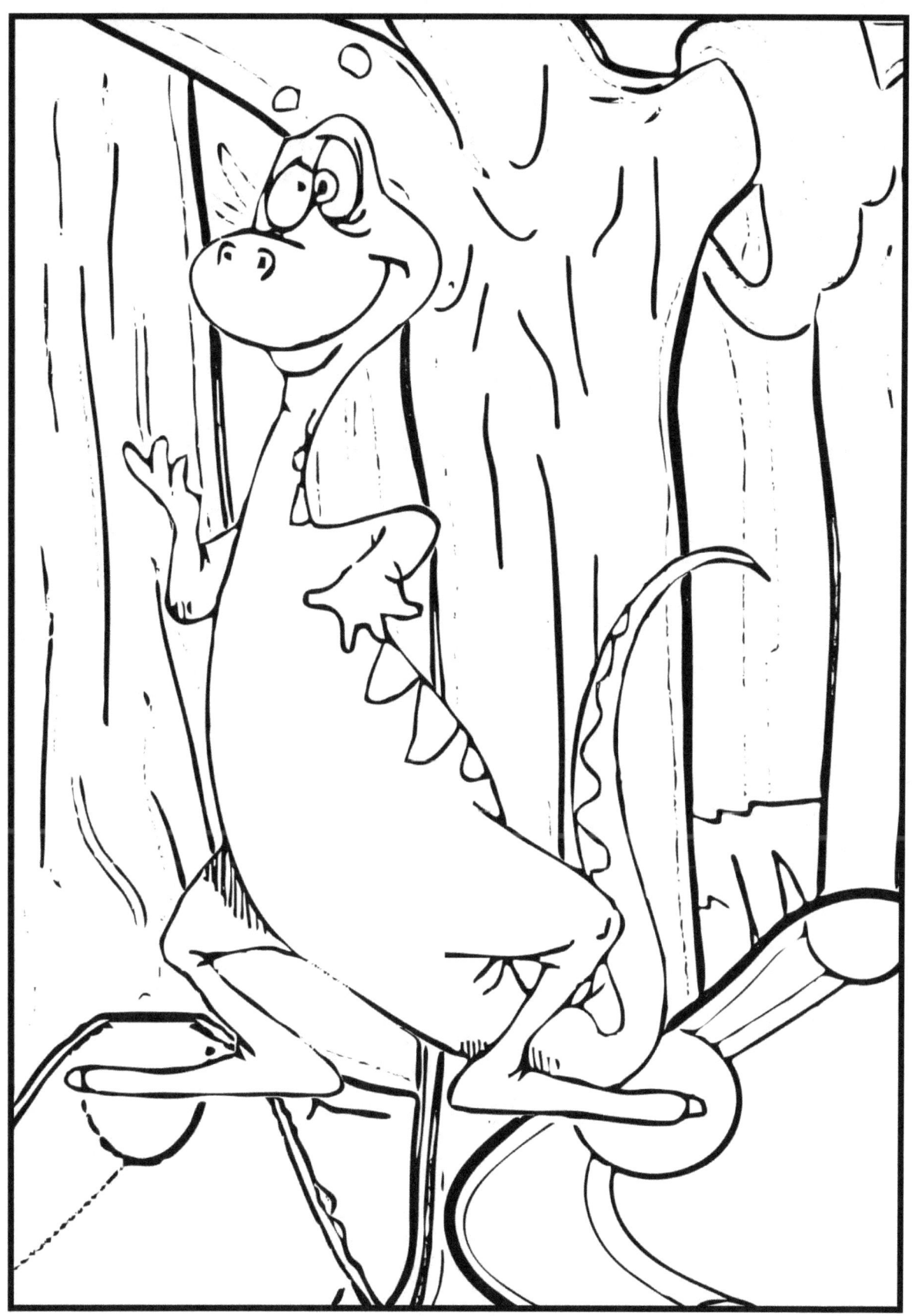

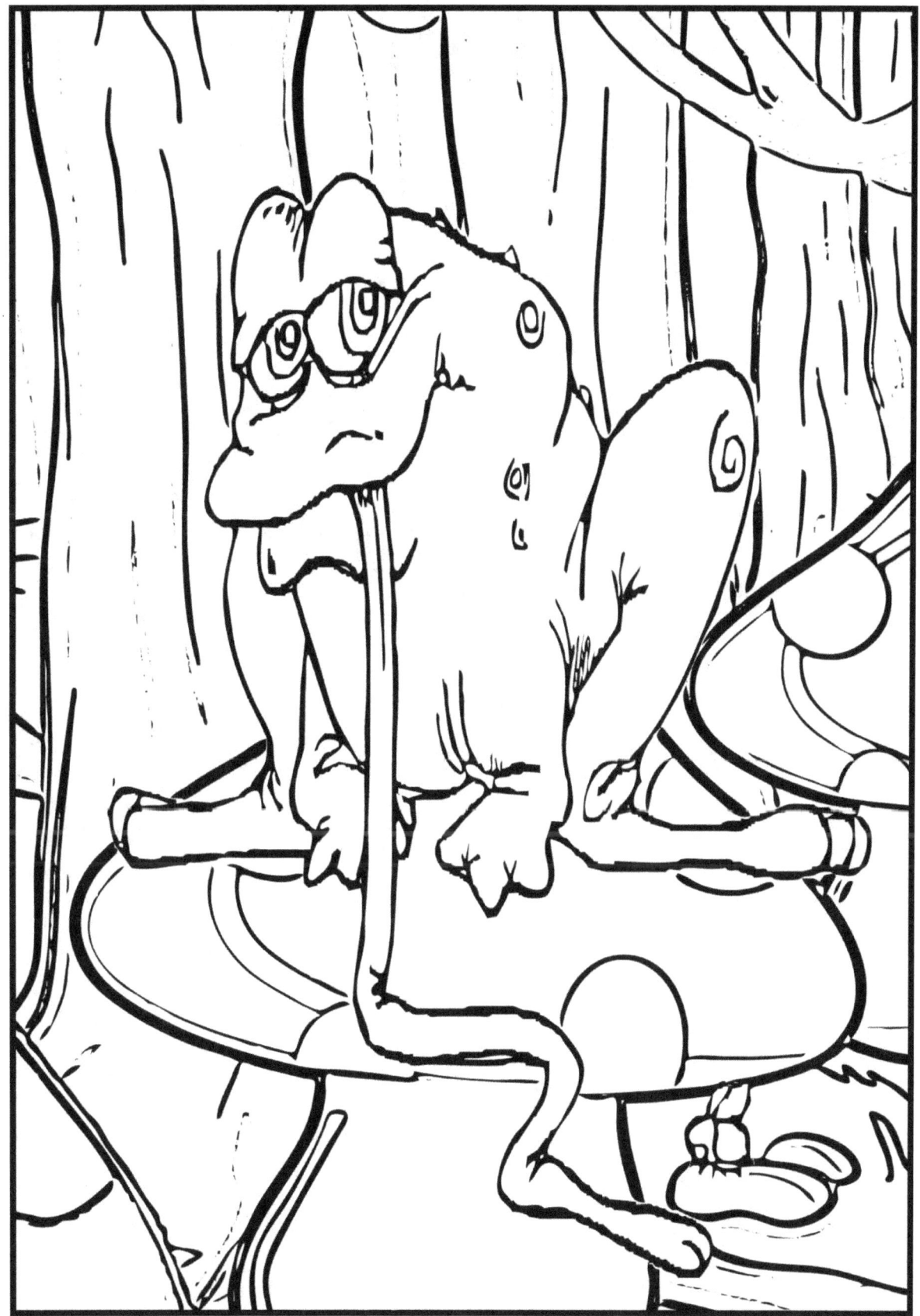

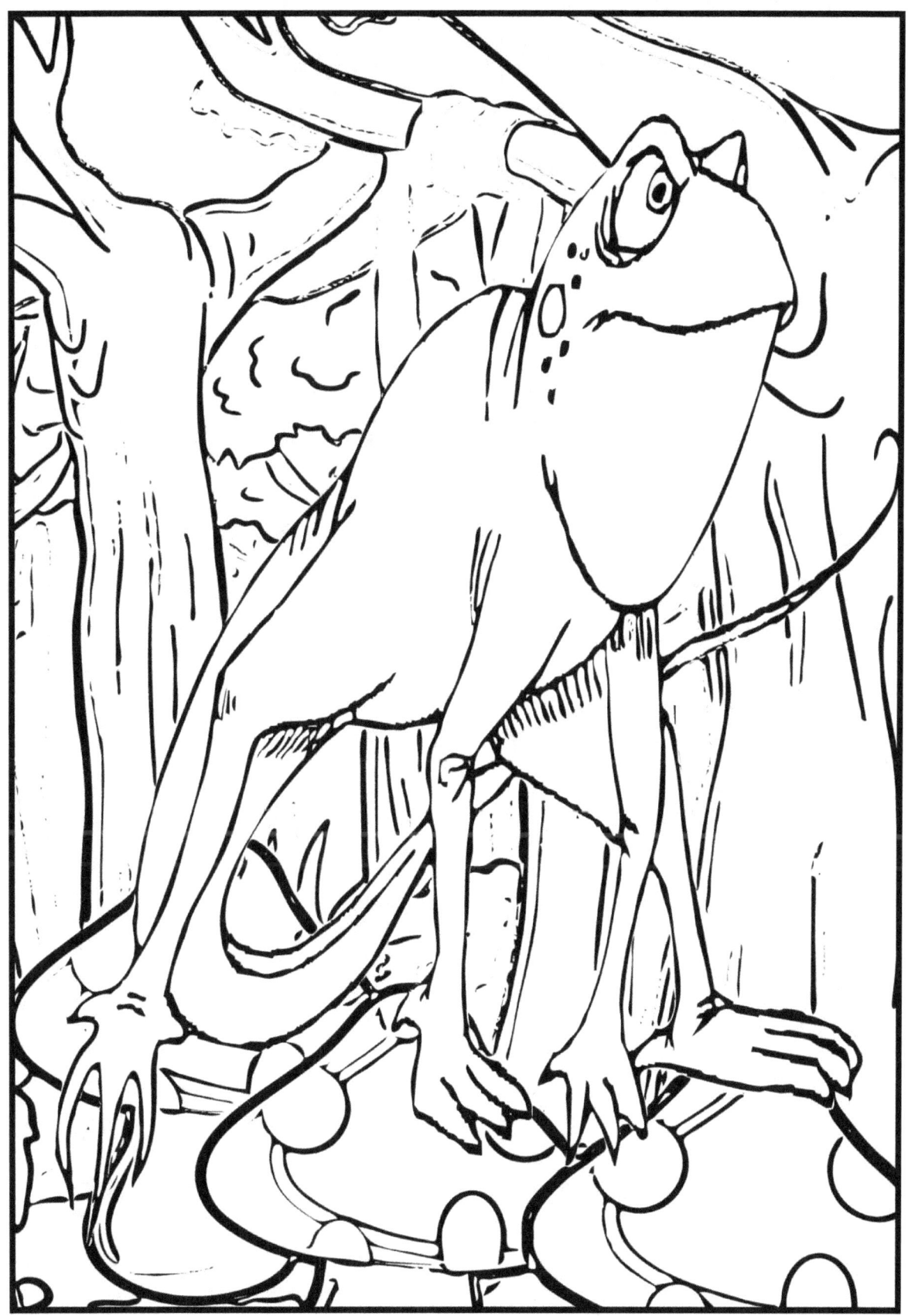

www.ingramcontent.com/pod-product-compliance
Lightning Source LLC
Chambersburg PA
CBHW081208180526
45170CB00006B/2262